PENGUI

THE PORTRA
SCREE

G000164474

Laura Jones has worked with Jane Campion on a previous film, the adaptation of Janet Frame's autobiography *An Angel at My Table*. She wrote the original screenplay for *High Tide*, directed by Gillian Armstrong, and two forthcoming feature films: *Oscar and Lucinda*, directed by Gillian Armstrong, based on the novel by Peter Carey, and *A Thousand Acres*, directed by Jocelyn Moorhouse, based on the novel by Jane Smiley. She lives in Sydney, Australia.

The *Portrait of a Lady*

Laura Jones

Screenplay based on
the novel by
Henry James

PENGUIN BOOKS

PENGUIN BOOKS

Published by the Penguin Group
Penguin Books Ltd, 27 Wrights Lane, London W8 5TZ, England
Penguin Books USA Inc., 375 Hudson Street, New York, New York 10014, USA
Penguin Books Australia Ltd, Ringwood, Victoria, Australia
Penguin Books Canada Ltd, 10 Alcorn Avenue, Toronto, Ontario, Canada M4V 3B2
Penguin Books (NZ) Ltd, 182–190 Wairau Road, Auckland 10, New Zealand

Penguin Books Ltd, Registered Offices: Harmondsworth, Middlesex, England

First published in the USA by Penguin Books 1996
First published in Great Britain by Penguin Books 1997
1 3 5 7 9 10 8 6 4 2

Printed in England by Clays Ltd, St Ives plc
Designed by Virginia Norey

Preface

The novel *The Portrait of a Lady* exists as a thing in itself, finished, complete. The film also does. But a screenplay, by the very fact of its function, can't exist in this way. It is always only one part, however crucial, of a process. It is a finished, complete object only for a short time: between the final writing and day one of production. Then it disappears into the whole.

Christopher Hampton writes in the introduction to his screenplay of *Dangerous Liaisons* that publishing the shooting script can seem like "a kind of reproach or criticism," so he chose to publish the script that reflected the final cut of the film.

I agonized over this question, seeing the beauty of reading exactly what was seen on screen, but also seeing the interest in reading a screenplay as part of the filmmaking process—from novel to screenplay to film. For the film student, this process, I hope, will be a valuable one, allowing all the pleasures of detective work. For the general reader, I hope it will not be confusing, but will serve to throw a light backwards onto the filmmaking process.

When Jane Campion first suggested adapting Henry James's *Portrait* to me, in my kitchen in Sydney, I had already read the novel and loved it. I was naturally also scared of the idea. The size and scope of the novel and its world; James's masterly, rich writing; the amount of dialogue: all these things seemed tantalizing and frightening at the same time.

To go from six hundred and something pages of highly detailed narrative with its great, subtle, bold dialogue and structure—the bricks all fitted together that James writes about in his Preface—"scrupulously fitted together and packed in"—to a screenplay of about 120 sparely laid-out pages, would seem like courting sacrilege. As a screenwriter, I had to have faith that the visual storytelling, the performances, and Jane's ability to deal with states of mind would fill in, fill up, elaborate, the shorthand version that is the screenplay on the page. In adapting from novel to screen, you empty out in order to fill up. The screenwriter has to have faith that the sparse words of the screenplay are a sturdy, inventive, and—at their best, to the director—inspirational signpost to the next stages in the making of the film.

Over a series of meetings, Jane and I talked about why we loved the novel and started to lay the ground for what *kind* of film it could be. I remember our working our way toward understanding Isabel, not only in her world, but for us in our own pasts and in our understanding of what it is like to be a girl like Isabel, in any time. We had to do what James had done, to understand Isabel as our "centre of consciousness."

For the purposes of film storytelling, I found the novel's narrative very clever and enticing. It is structured around two secrets and their revelations. The first, James allows us, but not Isabel, into. With the second secret, James chooses to keep both Isabel and us in the dark.

Allowing us into the first secret—the trap laid by Madame Merle and Osmond to capture Isabel and her fortune—lets us watch Isabel's journey out into the world with a sense of fear for her innocence, a desire for her to *know*, to discover, what we know: that she is being used. When will she see? The second secret James cleverly allows us to discover as Isabel discovers it. The doubling and reflecting of two opposites play out all the way through the novel: in its use of light and dark; benign and malign; trust and betrayal; money and its good and bad uses; the light of Isabel against Madame Merle's dark portrait of a lady. Ralph's light—the benign artist—giving Isabel the freedom of her imagination, against Osmond's dark spirit—the bad artist—who captures and deadens to perfection in his "house of dumbness, house of darkness." The state of Isabel's marriage mirrored back to her through the plans to marry Pansy to Lord Warburton at times felt like a maze I could never see the whole of. But I wanted to try to use the elegant reflecting structure that James used in the novel, turning Isabel into a detective of her own marriage. It was the most difficult part of the screenplay to write, probably as difficult as the opening sequences, before Madame Merle is introduced, and the dark plot is laid in Florence.

The ending presented itself as a dilemma. In the novel James writes that for Isabel there is a "very straight path back" to Rome. But he doesn't tell us what she does when she arrives there. I took a clue from a scene between Pansy and Isabel in the convent, when Isabel promises to return to Pansy, and wrote this return as the ending of the screenplay.

James wrote in his notebooks: "The obvious criticism

of course will be that it is not finished—that I have not seen the heroine to the end of her situation—that I have left her *en l'air* . . . the whole of anything is never told; you can only take what groups together" and, in the preface to his first novel, **Roderick Hudson**: "Really, universally, relations stop nowhere, and the exquisite problem of the artist is eternally but to draw, by a geometry of his own, the circle within which they shall happily appear to do so." The screenplay ending widens James's circle a little, stretches it a fraction with a clue from him, to show what Isabel does when she takes her "very straight path back" to Rome. This ending was shot and remained in the first few cuts of the film before Jane decided to draw the circle in tighter than James had. The novel's ending has caused a lot of argument among both readers and James scholars. For those people, both the screenplay's ending and the film's ending will be equally contentious, because it is not the Master's.

My involvement in the making of the film continued on into rehearsals, which were held in London in the big, old, unused town hall at Hampstead. This is where I heard the words of the screenplay read for the first time. Or read by someone other than Jane and myself. In Sydney, we had read through the script a number of times together, each taking various parts. Jane was a charming Isabel and cunning, lazy Osmond and I felt myself to be a natural Madame Merle. I excused any dud line as being a problem of performance, and Jane could hardly argue.

When I heard Isabel (Nicole Kidman) and Madame Merle (Barbara Hershey), Rosier (Christian Bale) and Pansy (Valentina Cervi), Ralph (Martin Donovan) and Caspar (Viggo Mortensen), and became a part of the intimate atmosphere that is created during rehearsals, I suppose I fell in love. I had already been in love with the novel and, in a way—although adored is maybe more the word—with James, and now I adored the actors. Their involvement mirrored mine, the journey I had taken in the writing. They claimed their characters, their words. They cared as much as I had about how and what their characters said and did. I felt enormous gratitude for their talent and their devotion to what we were making, with Jane as the great alchemist at the center of it all, creating a strange, intimate working life, drawing us all into the film she was cooking up.

I visited the location, for only a few days, in Rome. By this stage I felt totally irrelevant; the huge machinery of filmmaking had taken over. I did the classic thing of getting in a shot and having to be ordered out of it. Twice. I felt almost embarrassed that the words on the page, written at home in all kinds of domestic circumstances, had grown to these hundreds of people, all this equipment, this grand location at the Palazzo Farnese, and the art director Janet Patterson's detailed, beautiful, moody creation of the visual world of the film. It was here that I also saw John Malkovich's elegant, wonderfully inventive playing of Gilbert Osmond.

In the editing process, I have watched Jane at work, with Veronika Jenet, nipping and tucking, a stroke here, a stroke there, a broad sweep here and there, the process as plastic as that of writing the screenplay, all in the service of the story she wants to tell, the kind of film she is making. I want to write the kind of film that she is growing, because the sense of the process is very much like that. And, instead of feeling protective of words I wrote, dialogue or images or even structure, I have watched an artist at work, following her own instincts and knowledge, and I see that everything, including the screenplay, is used in a continuing, living sense, to arrive at the final moment of saying, "This is it."

And there is Henry James in his hotel room in Florence, overlooking the Arno, 117 years ago, starting to write *Portrait*. And there he is being booed in the theater in London at the first night of his play *Guy Domville*. And I hope that we have given him his theatrical desires: to be loved and understood as a dramatist, in performance. What he would have made of film, and the 1990s, I can barely guess, but if he is turning in his grave at the vision of Isabel's romantic sexual fantasies, I hope he is turning with pleasure.

Laura Jones
June 1996

Contents

The
Portrait of
a Lady

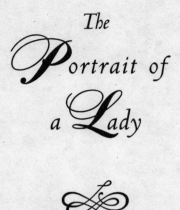

We move through:

A series of portraits—not stills but living, breathing young women.

Although we start in our time and end in the past, the young women have qualities vividly in common.

Independent, impatient, unacquainted with pain, a confidence at once innocent and dogmatic, spontaneous, full of theories, with delicate, desultory, flamelike spirits, facing their destinies.

Today's girl we see from top to toe, but as we go back in time, we move in closer and closer, until we have settled in intimate detail on the face of Isabel Archer. She could be today's girl, but happens to live in 1870.

Tiny sounds—of air in leaves, of distant voices, of a far-off dog barking, of heat lifting and settling in undergrowth—come to us.

I. *A thin veil of cloud must have passed across the sun: for a moment light and shade even out to a cool sameness. We see* **Isabel**

Archer fully: she is "undeniably spare, and ponderably light, and proveably tall."

Isabel's heightened feelings as she intensely reflects on the shock she has just experienced: although unwanted, it is disturbingly satisfying.

Isabel becomes conscious of the moment's darkening light before the cloud passes and the secluded, leafy little arbor is sunlit again.

Behind her, the weight of the lowest branches of an ancient tree are supported in the crooks of almost equally ancient uprights cut from tree boughs.

Behind the tree, unseen by *Isabel*, stands a pair of male legs, seen from below the knee, in riding breeches and spurred boots. The tree's foliage hides the owner of the boots.

Circling around the tree, we find the voyeur watching *Isabel* through the foliage is **Lord Warburton**——"handsome, fresh-colored, fair and frank, with a certain fortunate, brilliant, exceptional look."

He hesitates: to turn and leave or to advance?

Isabel, her back to him, on the stone bench: a little black piece in the green puzzle of leaves.

Warburton moves forward: branches, leaves crackle.

Isabel, startled, turns on the bench to see **Warburton** coming back into the arbor.

2

WARBURTON: There's one thing more, Miss Archer. You know, if you don't like Lockleigh—if you think it's damp or anything of that sort—you need never go within fifty miles of it. It's not damp, by the way. I've had the house thoroughly examined, it's perfectly safe and right. But if you shouldn't fancy it you needn't dream of living in it. There's no difficulty whatever about that, I have plenty of houses. I thought I'd just mention it. Some people don't like a moat, you know.

ISABEL: I adore a moat.

Warburton, grave, watching Isabel, conscious that maybe he won't succeed. His hands, held behind his back, give short nervous shakes to his riding crop.

WARBURTON: I'm very sure, you know. I don't go off easily, but when I'm touched, it's for life, Miss Archer.

2. *Just before the flood of summer light begins to fade, across perfect velvet lawns, in deep shade under ancient oaks and beeches, a little tea party is in progress.*

*A **butler** carries another pot of hot water across lawns.*

*Persian rugs, cushioned seats, books and papers furnish the tea spot. **Dogs** loll in velvety shade. A **collie** keeps an eye on old **Mr. Touchett**—"dressed in well-brushed black, with his look of contented shrewdness"—holding his large, brilliantly painted teacup,* *shawl slipping off knees, feet in embroidered slippers, in his invalid's mechanical chair.*

*Three of the wicker chairs empty: Lord Warburton's large white hat and soiled dogskin gloves thrown down on one, Isabel's parasol on another; the third belongs to **Ralph Touchett**—"tall, lean and loosely put together, with a sickly, witty, charming face, clever and ill"—who wanders, bending to tuck in his father's shawl.*

*Warburton's sisters, the two **Misses Molyneux**—with their extreme sweetness and shyness of manner, in matching sealskin jackets—watch everything with their round, contented eyes.*

***Bunchie**, Ralph's rowdy little terrier, breaks the idle mood as he runs out of tea-party shade with a volley of shrill barks.*

*Our little group watches Bunchie racing across the lawns towards **Isabel**.*

MISS MOLYNEUX 1: Here is Miss Archer.
MISS MOLYNEUX 2: No, she is going up to the house.
MISS MOLYNEUX 1: So she is.

*And indeed, instead of returning to the tea party, **Isabel** is making her way up the slope towards the sunlit back of the house.*

*The **Misses Molyneux** are further puzzled as they see their brother, **Lord Warburton**, coming towards them from another direction.*

*Bunchie trots beside **Isabel**, who points back to the tea party:*

ISABEL: No, Bunchie, go back. Back.

But naughty Bunchie won't listen, and, barely pausing:

ISABEL: Oh, you naughty hound.

Isabel bends in one pliant movement and scoops up the little dog and for a brief second holds him up face to face, shaking him, growling back at him, to his delight; then tucks him under her arm and disappears into the house.

Ralph sees that Warburton is apparently very upset and distracted: he has never seen his friend so socially awkward.

RALPH: Some more tea? There is fresh hot water—
WARBURTON: No, Touchett, thank you, I can't. If my sisters are ready—

The two Misses Molyneux stand, like ladies-in-waiting, as War-burton retrieves his hat and gloves.

3. *From an upstairs window: long, goldeny-dark twilight spreads across Gardencourt grounds and down to the river.*

Mr. Touchett's collie walks beside wheels of a complicated mechanical chair as Ralph wheels his father to the open window. Both are dressed for dinner. A nearby table is piled high with books and journals, newspapers, and letters.

Ralph's pack of hounds wait to see what their master will do.

RALPH: Shall I sit with you until dinner, Daddy?

MR. TOUCHETT: I would like that, but Isabel has asked if she may (talk to me)—

And Isabel is in the doorway.

MR. TOUCHETT: Ah, here she is. Come in, my dear. Sit here.

Ralph can't help searching Isabel's face for what has happened, as he passes her, dogs following, out of the room.

Isabel sits opposite her uncle.

ISABEL: Uncle, I ought to let you know that Lord Warburton has asked me to marry him.

MR. TOUCHETT: Well, I told you you'd be a success over here. Americans are highly appreciated, and you're very beautiful, you know.

ISABEL (*nervous laugh*): Oh yes, of course, I'm lovely!

MR. TOUCHETT: Do you mind telling me whether you accepted him?

ISABEL: I know it seems tasteless and ungrateful, but I can't marry him.

MR. TOUCHETT: You didn't find his offer sufficiently attractive?

Isabel becomes ardent in her theorizing:

ISABEL: It was attractive; there was one moment when I would have given my little finger to say yes. But I think I have to begin by getting a general impression of life, do you see? And there's a light that has to dawn. I can't explain it, but I know it's there. I know I can't give up. I'm not afraid, you know.

MR. TOUCHETT: No, I guessed you weren't.

ISABEL: The great point's to be happy. That's what I came to Europe for, to be as happy as possible.

MR. TOUCHETT: Well, of course an old man can't judge for a young lady, but I'm glad you didn't ask me before you made up your mind. He's a very fine man. He has a hundred thousand a year, half a dozen houses to live in, and a seat in Parliament as I have one at my own dinner table.

ISABEL: I hope very much I have no more offers.

*As **Isabel** looks out across the park in the deepening twilight, her uncle watches her with his shrewd, speculative, benevolent gaze.*

ISABEL: They upset me completely!

Isabel bursts into tears. The collie whines and lays his head on her knees.

4. *Morning light floods into an upstairs bedroom where **Mrs. Touchett**, Isabel's aunt—a dry, humorous, elderly woman "whose face has a good deal of rather violent point"—watches **Isabel**'s preparations for her trip to London with little favor.*

Isabel going through her clothes hanging in wardrobe:

7

ISABEL: . . . This . . . and this . . . this one . . .

*A **maid** takes out the garments and lays them on the bed, where hats and other clothes are laid out. Bunchie, on the bed among them, watches the activity. The **maid** gathers shoes and leaves the room.*

MRS. TOUCHETT: Your uncle is right—you certainly can't go to London without an escort.

ISABEL: My friend Henrietta will be with me.

MRS. TOUCHETT: Your friend sounds very Bohemian. No doubt she will want to stay in a "boarding house." Ralph has put you down at his club. With Ralph you may go anywhere.

ISABEL: Isn't anything proper here?

MRS. TOUCHETT: You're too fond of your own ways.

ISABEL: Yes, I'm very fond of them.

MRS. TOUCHETT: I don't expect you to heed my advice, but as you have neither mother nor father, I do expect you to listen to it.

Isabel has changed her mind about a number of garments on bed and has returned them to wardrobe and chosen new ones.

MRS. TOUCHETT: I may as well tell you that your uncle has informed me of your relations with Lord Warburton.

ISABEL: They're hardly relations. He has seen me but three or four times.

MRS. TOUCHETT: Why did you tell your uncle rather than me?

ISABEL: Because he knows Lord Warburton better.

MRS. TOUCHETT: Yes, but you're my niece, and I know you better.

8

ISABEL (*smiles*): I'm not sure of that.

MRS. TOUCHETT: Nor am I, after all. Especially when you give me that rather conceited look. One would think you were awfully pleased with yourself and had carried off a prize. I suppose that when you refuse an English lord it's because you expect to do something better.

ISABEL: Ah, my uncle didn't say that!

The maid has returned with a manservant carrying boxes and cases for London.

5. *The tag end of summer in the half-empty city.*

Isabel and Ralph in one of the carriages that pass under the trees of a great park.

For Ralph, Isabel's arrival "is an open-handed gift of fate" that has lifted his melancholy.

Isabel is looking out of the carriage as it stops. Curious Ralph leans forward to follow her gaze:

Henrietta Stackpole on the National Gallery steps, "framed" in the carriage window: a portrait of a young woman "as crisp and new and comprehensive as a first issue before the folding. From top to toe she has no misprint."

RALPH: Shall I love your friend or shall I hate her?

ISABEL: Whichever you do will matter very little to Henrietta. She doesn't care a straw what men think of her.

RALPH: Will she interview me?

ISABEL: She'll not think you important enough.

6.   *Elizabeth I straddles a globe of the world. The wives of Henry VIII and other Tudor portraits hang three-deep.*

The cool shadowy rooms of the National Portrait Gallery almost empty: a cluster of German tourists with their guide; a student copying at an easel; a few others strolling with their Baedekers.

Ralph, mooching alone, keeps an endlessly fascinated eye on Isabel, who is pursued by Henrietta further down the gallery.

Isabel walks slowly down a wall of portraits, stopping every now and then to examine a painting. Henrietta hard on her heels, interested only in Isabel.

HENRIETTA: When I wrote to you from Liverpool I said I had something particular to tell you. You haven't asked me what it is. Is it because you've suspected?

Isabel, absorbed in a portrait, disappoints Henrietta with her casual answer:

ISABEL: Suspected what? What have you to tell me?

HENRIETTA: You don't ask that right. Mr. Goodwood came out in the steamer with me.

Isabel, disturbed, now looks at her friend.

ISABEL: Ah!
HENRIETTA: You say *that* right. He has come after you.
ISABEL: Did he tell you so?
HENRIETTA: No, he told me nothing, but I spoke of you a good deal.
ISABEL: I'm sorry you did that.
HENRIETTA: It was a pleasure to me, and I liked the way he listened. He was so quiet, so intense, he drank it all in.
ISABEL: He thinks too well of me already. He oughtn't to be encouraged.
HENRIETTA: He's dying for a little encouragement. I see his face now, and his look while I talked. I never saw an ugly man look so handsome.
ISABEL: He's very simple-minded. And he's not so ugly.
HENRIETTA: You certainly encouraged him.

Isabel is about to deny this, but she falters under her friend's implacable scrutiny.

ISABEL: Yes, it's true, I did encourage him.
HENRIETTA: He'll find you changed. You're not the girl you were a few short weeks ago.
ISABEL: I hope he'll hate me.

7. *In the Tower of London, the somber thick-walled Norman interior of the massive White Tower overshadows our little party.*

Ralph idly ambles around the walls with his hands in his pockets.

Henrietta, notebook and pencil idle, watches him for quite a while: he presents himself to her as an irritating problem to be solved.

HENRIETTA: Does your cousin go around all day with his hands in his pockets? What does he do for a living?
ISABEL: He's terribly ill. He's quite unfit for work.
HENRIETTA: Don't you believe it. I work when I'm sick. I should like to show him up. He would make a beautiful specimen—the Alienated American.
ISABEL: He would die of it! Henrietta?

But Henrietta has already bustled away from Isabel and followed Ralph, bailing him up in the doorway of a tiny cell.

HENRIETTA: What do they think of you over here?
RALPH: They delight in me.
HENRIETTA: That's because you truckle to them.
RALPH: Set it down a little to my natural charm.
HENRIETTA: I don't know anything about your natural charm. If you've got any charm it's quite unnatural. It's a charm I don't appreciate, anyway. Why don't you make yourself useful in some way? You're afraid of meeting my eye.
RALPH: No—excuse me— (*Calls*) Bantling!

Bob Bantling—"a stout, sleek, smiling man of forty"—turns and sees Ralph.

BANTLING: Touchett!
RALPH: Allow me to introduce Miss Stackpole. Miss

Stackpole, Mr. Bantling. Miss Stackpole takes notes, Bantling. She's a great satirist. She sees through us all and works us up for her articles.

*Henrietta has held out her hand to **Bantling**, who laughs immoderately as he takes it.*

8.   *Winchester Square in dusky stillness of late-summer twilight. Street lamps not yet lit, nor lights on in houses around the square. The little center garden a darkening green oasis.*

*Isabel and **Ralph** climb the steps of one of the houses and disappear through the door, held open by a **manservant**.*

9.   *The Winchester Square house closed up for summer: dust-sheeted, some rugs taken up, only one big dusky room half-settled, where Ralph has made a little camp.*

*Isabel sits in armchair while **Ralph** opens a window to the evening——the stillness broken by an occasional footstep from outside.*

RALPH: If you'll permit me, I'll light a cigarette.
ISABEL: You may do what you please, if you'll amuse me until seven-thirty.

Ralph lights his cigarette and sits in armchair opposite Isabel. In the unlit room, Ralph "likes immensely being alone with Isabel in the thickening dusk; it made her seem to depend on him and to be in his power."

RALPH: Tell me this, what had you in mind when you refused Warburton?

Ralph sees Isabel suppress a start.

RALPH: I have his leave to let you know he has told me.
ISABEL: Did he ask you to talk to me?
RALPH: No, not that. He told me because he couldn't help it. We're old friends, and he was very heavy-hearted.
ISABEL: What had I in mind when I refused him?
RALPH: What was the logic that indicated so remarkable an act?
ISABEL: Why do you call it remarkable?
RALPH: As a man, Warburton has hardly a fault.
ISABEL: I refused him because he was too perfect, then.
RALPH: That's ingenious rather than candid. Perhaps you don't know how he has been stalked.
ISABEL: I don't wish to know.
RALPH: I pity him.
ISABEL: Why, that seems to me his only fault, that one can't pity him a little. He appears to have everything, to know everything, to be everything.

The glowing tip, the faint smoke from Ralph's cigarette. The room gradually darkening.

RALPH: If you've really given Warburton his final answer, I'm rather glad it has been what it was. I don't mean I'm glad for you, and still less of course for him. I'm glad for myself.

ISABEL: Are you thinking of proposing to me?

RALPH: What I mean is that I shall have the thrill of seeing what a young lady does who won't marry Lord Warburton.

ISABEL: You asked about logic, I'll tell you. It's that I can't escape my fate.

RALPH: Your fate?

ISABEL: It's not my fate to give up.

RALPH: Do you call marrying Lord Warburton "giving up"?

ISABEL: It's getting—getting a great deal. But it's giving up other chances.

RALPH: Chances for what?

ISABEL: I don't mean chances to marry. From life, from the usual chances and dangers.

RALPH: You've answered my question.

ISABEL: It seems to me I've told you very little.

RALPH: You've told me the great thing: that the world interests you and that you want to throw yourself into it.

ISABEL: I never said that.

RALPH: I think you meant it. Don't repudiate it. It's so fine!

ISABEL: I don't know what you're trying to fasten upon me.

Isabel stands, *Ralph* following. *They look at each other in the dusk: "exchange a gaze—full of utterances too vague for words."*

ISABEL: It's getting very dark, I must go.

10. *A cluster of **onlookers** around a giant **strongman**, his almost naked body oiled and gleaming, bound around with a maze of chains, under street lamps. His **spruiker** shouting his charge's strength to the crowd.*

*A **passing figure** catches our attention: moving quickly and with purpose, he ignores the sideshow, passes by, and turns the corner into Park Place.*

His swift steps up marble stairs.

*A **doorman** opens the door and **Caspar Goodwood**—a young, tall, dark, and angular American Prince—passes through the door into the lit interior of Pratt's Club.*

11. *Lamplight, discarded books, the remains of a solitary light dinner, in Isabel's upstairs sitting room at Pratt's.*

Isabel and Caspar face each other in a state of contention.

ISABEL: How did you know I was here?
CASPAR: Miss Stackpole let me know.
ISABEL (*bitter*): That is not kind of her.
CASPAR: You said you hoped never to hear from me

again, I know that. But I never accepted any such rule as my own.

ISABEL: I didn't say I hoped *never* to hear from you.

CASPAR: Not for five years then, for ten years, twenty years. It's the same thing.

Isabel bursts out:

ISABEL: What good do you expect to get by insisting?

CASPAR (*gloomy*): I disgust you very much.

Isabel sees that perfect frankness is her best weapon.

ISABEL: Yes, you don't at all delight me. You don't fit in, not in any way, just now. Think of me or not, only leave me alone.

CASPAR: Until when?

ISABEL: Well, for a year or two.

CASPAR: Which do you mean? Between one year and two there's all the difference in the world.

ISABEL: Call it two then.

CASPAR: You'll marry someone else as sure as I stand here.

ISABEL: I really don't want to marry. I shall probably never do it.

Isabel serious, passionately positive:

ISABEL: If you hear a rumor that I'm on the point of marrying, remember what I've told you and doubt it.

CASPAR: I hate to lose sight of you.

ISABEL: You're very angry.

CASPAR: Oh yes, I'm angry. I plead guilty to that.

*He puts out his hand. She takes it and they stand looking at each other for a moment, **Isabel** almost tender in her victory, before their hands separate. **Isabel** goes to the door of her bedroom, hand on doorknob, waiting for him to go, but he doesn't move.*

ISABEL: Goodbye.
CASPAR: In two years, then.

12.   *Isabel's bedroom dark except for a vague radiance thrown in from the club's court.*

Isabel comes in, shuts the door. She can make out the dim shapes of furniture, the gleam of the mirror.

After a while she hears the sound of Caspar leaving. She stands still a moment longer: the enjoyment she has in exercising her power is exhilarating. She is trembling, trying to resist her excitement.

*Isabel has refused two ardent suitors, and although she has done what is truest to her theories about liberty, she entertains **Caspar Goodwood**, **Lord Warburton**, and **Ralph**, who now appear in her fantasies.*

———

13. *A wilderness of tables in breakfast room at Pratt's, where* **Henrietta** *helps herself from the sideboard while keeping an eager eye out for* **Isabel.**

Isabel comes in to the breakfast room and crosses to **Henrietta,** *angry with her friend for setting a trap.*

ISABEL: You acted very wrongly.

HENRIETTA: You don't mean to tell me that you sent him off?

ISABEL: I asked him to leave me alone and I ask you the same, Henrietta.

Isabel, her warning given, goes to a table, **Henrietta** *following.*

HENRIETTA: Isabel Archer, if you marry one of these people I'll never speak to you again.

ISABEL: You had better wait till I'm asked.

HENRIETTA: Oh, you'll be asked quick enough, once you get off on the Continent. Annie Climber was asked three times in Italy—poor plain little Annie.

ISABEL: Well, if Annie Climber wasn't captured why should I be?

HENRIETTA: I don't believe Annie was pressed, but you'll be. Do you know where you're going, Isabel Archer?

ISABEL: No, and I find it very pleasant not to know.

HENRIETTA: You're drifting to some great mistake. You make me shudder!

Ralph, his usual mooching, ironic manner completely absent, comes into the breakfast room, looking for **Isabel.**

*He crosses to her and **Henrietta**.*

RALPH: My father has had an attack of his old malady. It's severe, I'm afraid.

*He has handed a telegram to **Isabel**, who reads it.*

RALPH: I've judged it best to see the doctor, Sir Matthew Hope, first. By great good luck he's in town, and I shall make sure of his coming down to Gardencourt.

***Isabel** is already standing:*

ISABEL: I shall go with you. I'll pack now.

*She hurries from the breakfast room, leaving **Ralph** and **Henrietta** to make their slower way out of the room.*

HENRIETTA: Isabel tells me that your father's a grand old man. I'm sorry I shall not be at Gardencourt. If it's really to be the last, I should so like to commemorate the closing scene.
RALPH (*dry*): My father may live a long time yet.

As they make their way out, through a maze of narrow, winding corridors:

HENRIETTA: I'm not at peace about Isabel. I fear she's going to marry one of these Europeans and I want to prevent it.
RALPH: What a rage you have for organizing people.

They come out into Pratt's lobby, with its big armchairs, little tables, and newspapers, and cross to the reception desk, where Ralph arranges the bill.

HENRIETTA: I want her to marry Mr. Caspar Goodwood. He's followed her out here from Boston. He was here, last night.

RALPH: Here? In Pratt's?

HENRIETTA: It was a little plot of mine.

RALPH: Is she very fond of him?

HENRIETTA: If she isn't she ought to be. He's simply wrapped up in her. Three months ago she gave him every reason to suppose he was acceptable to her, and it's not worthy of Isabel to go back on a friend simply because she has changed the scene.

RALPH: Isabel was cruel?

HENRIETTA: She gave him no satisfaction. Her only idea was to get rid of him.

RALPH: Poor Mr. Goodwood.

HENRIETTA: You don't say that as if you felt it.

*For **Ralph** this news of Isabel's refusal of yet another suitor only confirms his hopes, fires his imagination, for Isabel's future.*

14. *Gardencourt now a house of sickness, with the perceptible hush that precedes a crisis.*

Isabel wanders, book in hand, Bunchie clicking behind. She passes a window and we stay to look out at:

Misty rain washing the damp, chill grounds.

Isabel passes the foot of the stairs and we see:

The London doctor **Sir Matthew Hope** going upstairs with **Mrs. Touchett** and a **nurse**.

In a corridor **Isabel** is overtaken by a **second nurse**, carrying a sickroom tray piled with medical things.

In the **second nurse**'s chinking wake **Isabel** hears, faintly, the sound of a piano being played.

Puzzled, she follows the sound of the music through the house; it grows louder, until:

She stops on the threshold of the drawing room, the music flowing out.

15.   *Isabel* looks down the long distance of the drawing room:

A strange **woman**, her back to **Isabel**, plays the piano with great skill and feeling.

Isabel moves into the room, unnoticed by the stranger, and sits, drawn into the music.

As the music continues, **Isabel** watches out of the windows:

The rain, now begun in earnest, washing the cold-looking lawn, the wind shaking the great trees.

*The music finishes and **Isabel** stands.*

*The stranger—**Serena Merle**: "forty years old, charming, sympathetic, intelligent, cultivated and wonderfully dressed"—turns quickly, as if just aware of **Isabel's** presence.*

*They take each other in, in a brief, comprehensive minute. **Isabel** dazzled as she moves down the room towards the stranger.*

ISABEL: That's very beautiful, and your playing makes it more beautiful still.

MADAME MERLE: You don't think I disturbed Mr. Touchett, then? His room is so far away, and I played just —just *du bout des doigts.*

ISABEL: I should think that to hear such lovely music would make him feel better.

MADAME MERLE: I am afraid there are moments in life when even Schubert has nothing to say to us.

ISABEL: Would you play something more?

MADAME MERLE: If it will give you pleasure, delighted.

*__Madame Merle__ turns back to piano while **Isabel** sits near her. She strikes a few chords, then turns:*

MADAME MERLE: Are you the niece, the young American?

ISABEL: I'm my aunt's niece.

MADAME MERLE: *C'est bon.* We're compatriots. I'm Madame Merle.

*And she begins to play. **Isabel** watches her, drawn into the enchanting mood she creates, helped by the Schubert and the room cocooned from the stormy day outside.*

16. *Evening of the same stormy day.*

*A fire burns in **Mr. Touchett**'s sickroom. A table of medical things.*

***Mrs. Touchett** leaves the room, her watch over.*

***Ralph** by his father's bed. The collie keeps guard at foot of bed. In the silence, the old man's labored breathing, the faint sound of gusty wind and rain. Room slowly darkening.*

***Ralph** stares down tenderly at his father; they have been best friends.*

After quite a while the old man opens his eyes.

MR. TOUCHETT: Who's that with me? Is it my son?

RALPH: Yes, it's your son, Daddy.

MR. TOUCHETT: And is there no one else?

RALPH: No one else.

MR. TOUCHETT: I want to talk a little.

RALPH: Won't it tire you?

MR. TOUCHETT: It won't matter if it does. I shall have a long rest. I want to talk about you.

RALPH: You had better select a brighter topic.

MR. TOUCHETT: You're a bright enough topic for me.

The best thing you can do, when I'm gone, will be to marry.

Ralph sits back, returns his father's appealing gaze.

MR. TOUCHETT: What do you think of your cousin?

Ralph starts, his smile strained.

RALPH: Do I understand you to propose that I should marry Isabel?
MR. TOUCHETT: Well, that's what it comes to in the end. Don't you like Isabel?
RALPH: Yes, very much.

He stands, wanders to window, looks out, unseeing.

RALPH: I like Isabel very much.
MR. TOUCHETT: I have thought a great deal about it.
RALPH: So have I. I don't mind telling you that.

He returns to the bedside.

MR. TOUCHETT: You are in love with her, then? I should think you would be. It's as if she came over on purpose.
RALPH: No, I'm not in love with her, but I should be if —if certain things were different.
MR. TOUCHETT: Things are always different from what they might be.

*A long, meditative pause, as if **Ralph** is gathering courage.*

RALPH: I shall not live many years, but I hope I shall live long enough to see what Isabel does with herself. I should like to do something for her.

MR. TOUCHETT: What do you mean by that?

RALPH: She wants to see the world, for instance. I should like to put money in her purse.

MR. TOUCHETT: I've thought of that, too. I've left her a legacy, five thousand pounds.

RALPH: That's capital, it's very kind of you. But I should like to do a little more.

Mr. Touchett waits while Ralph pauses.

RALPH: I should like to make her rich.

MR. TOUCHETT: What do you mean by "rich"?

RALPH: I call people rich when they're able to meet the requirements of their imagination.

MR. TOUCHETT: To do what she likes with?

RALPH: Absolutely what she likes.

They stare at each other, deeply, for quite a while. Ralph thinks his father has given up the attempt to follow him. But finally:

MR. TOUCHETT: Tell me this. Doesn't it occur to you that a young lady with a fortune may fall a victim to the fortune hunters?

RALPH: She'll hardly fall a victim to more than one.

MR. TOUCHETT: Well, one's too many.

RALPH: Decidedly. That's a risk, but I think it's small, and I'm prepared to take it. But Daddy, it's scandalous the way I've tired you.

He leans over his father, smoothing his pillows.

17. *Mrs.* **Touchett** *and the great doctor,* **Sir Matthew Hope,** *dressed for dinner, in front of the drawing-room fireplace.*

Across the room, **Isabel** *follows* **Ralph** *as he comes in. As she hurries to stop him:*

ISABEL: Who is this Madame Merle?

RALPH: She's the one person in the world whom my mother very much admires. If she were not herself, which she after all very much prefers, she would like to be Madame Merle.

ISABEL: Well, she's very charming, and she plays beautifully.

RALPH: She does everything beautifully. She's complete.

Isabel studies Ralph.

ISABEL: You don't like her.

RALPH: On the contrary, I was once in love with her.

ISABEL: And she didn't care for you and that's why you don't like her.

RALPH: How can we have discussed such things? Monsieur Merle was then living.

ISABEL: Is he dead now?

RALPH: So she says.

ISABEL: Don't you believe her?

RALPH: Yes, because the husband of Madame Merle would be likely to pass away.

Madame Merle has come in behind Isabel and Ralph, rustling, smiling, fastening a bracelet.

They turn to her, and Isabel watches as Ralph offers her his arm.

18.   *Ancient oaks and beeches, their great swags of leaves soughing backwards and forwards in windy gusts of light drizzle.*

Across Gardencourt grounds, in the distance: Madame Merle and Isabel, under two umbrellas, turn into the gates of Gardencourt's long avenue.

They walk as close together as their two umbrellas will allow, in softest rain. Both good walkers, in their overcoats and neat stout boots.

MADAME MERLE: Americans certainly make poor Europeans—we've no natural place here. But a woman, it seems to me, has no natural place anywhere. Wherever she finds herself, she has to remain on the surface and more or less crawl.
ISABEL: I shall never crawl.
MADAME MERLE: Yes, on the whole I don't see you crawling.

A burst of heavier rain forces them to shelter under the thick canopy of a giant tree.

MADAME MERLE: But the men, the Americans. Look at poor Ralph Touchett—what sort of figure do you call that? Fortunately he has consumption. I say "fortunately" because it gives him something to do. His consumption's his *carrière*, it's a kind of position. Without that who would he be?

ISABEL: If he were not ill, he'd do something. He'd take his father's place in the bank.

MADAME MERLE: I doubt it. He's not at all fond of the bank.

The rain eases and they return to the path.

ISABEL: Are you not good friends?

MADAME MERLE: Perfectly, but he doesn't like me.

ISABEL: What have you done to him?

MADAME MERLE: Nothing whatever. But one has no need of a reason for that.

ISABEL: For not liking you? I think one has need of a very good reason.

MADAME MERLE: You're very kind. Be sure you have one ready for the day you begin.

ISABEL: Begin to dislike you? I shall never begin.

MADAME MERLE: I hope not, because if you do, you may never end.

The house comes into sight.

19. *The two figures under their umbrellas make their way towards the house, watched by:*

Ralph, *at library windows, hands in pockets. His gaze half critical, half rueful.*

20. *Watercolors and drawings of Scottish fens and a castle, of an Italian courtyard, of Gardencourt in this rainy summer week.*

We see them as **Isabel** *inspects Madame Merle's portfolio.*

Madame Merle *is checking her pieces of luggage in her room. She stops for a second and stares at the girl, unaware of her gaze, bent over the portfolio.*

MADAME MERLE: I'd give a good deal to be your age again.

Isabel, *startled by this bitter tone, looks up.*

MADAME MERLE: If only I could begin again—if I could have my life before me.
ISABEL: Your life's before you yet.
MADAME MERLE: No, the best part's gone, and gone for nothing.
ISABEL: Surely not for nothing.
MADAME MERLE: Why not—what have I got? Neither

husband, nor child, nor fortune, nor the traces of a beauty that I never had.

ISABEL: What should you like to do that you've not done?

Madame Merle flicks through her portfolio. After a pause:

MADAME MERLE: I'm very ambitious!

ISABEL: To me, you're a vivid image of success.

MADAME MERLE: My dreams were so great. I should make myself ridiculous by talking of them.

She holds out a watercolor of Gardencourt.

MADAME MERLE: I should like you to have this. I am going to six places in succession, but I shall see no one I like so well as you.

*Isabel takes the watercolor and, for thanks, kisses **Madame Merle**.*

21. *Ralph, at the fireplace in his father's sickroom, looks across to:*

Isabel sitting by his father's bed.

Mr. Touchett, in and out of consciousness, his face pulled this way and that, with little twitches and tics.

Isabel's attention deepens as his eyes open and he looks straight at her. She believes for a second he will recognize her, talk to her, say something important.

But instead, his mouth pulls wide open in a giant yawn. His eyes remain on **Isabel**, *uncomprehending*.

22. *Isabel* in the deep window-seat of the library, an unread book in her hands, Bunchie curled beside her.

She idly looks out of the library window, which is at right angles to the entrance front of the house.

The doctor's brougham waits at the entrance. The **doctor, Sir Matthew Hope**, followed by a **nurse** carrying his bag, comes out . . . draws on his gloves . . . checks his horse's knees . . . takes his bag from the **nurse** . . . gets into the brougham . . . drives away . . . all details seen as if time suspended.

A great, profound stillness descends.

After a while: slow, soft footsteps on carpet.

Isabel, almost startled, turns to see:

Ralph, hands in pockets, but his usual latent smile absolutely gone.

Isabel stands: her movement and glance are a question.

RALPH: Yes . . . it's all over . . . my father died an hour ago . . .
ISABEL: Ah, my poor Ralph!

She puts out both hands to him.

23.   *Drifts of autumn leaves being swept by a **servant** from the steps of the Touchetts' London house.*

Madame Merle comes up the steps and glances in passing at a large black sign with white lettering announcing that the house is for sale.

24.   *Uncurtained windows allow light to pour into the house, which is almost cleared of furniture; rugs have been rolled, pictures are stacked, **auction house representatives** are labelling and tagging, and **servants** are busy dismantling and wrapping and packing—much activity.*

*Mrs. Touchett, in mourning black, moves briskly through the rooms with **Madame Merle**.*

MRS. TOUCHETT: He has left me this house, but naturally I shall not live in it. I've a much better one in Florence. Ralph, of course, has Gardencourt.

The room where Ralph and Isabel sat in the dusk is now Mrs. Touchett's headquarters.

MRS. TOUCHETT: There's one remarkable clause in my husband's will. I'll ring for tea.

Madame Merle sits in Isabel's chair as Mrs. Touchett rings a bell.

MRS. TOUCHETT: He has left my niece a fortune.
MADAME MERLE: A fortune!
MRS. TOUCHETT: Isabel steps into something like seventy thousand pounds.

Madame Merle is transfixed; then:

MADAME MERLE: The clever creature!
MRS. TOUCHETT: What do you mean by that?

Madame Merle has only a second's awkwardness.

MADAME MERLE: It certainly is clever to achieve such results—without an effort.
MRS. TOUCHETT: There assuredly was no effort. Don't call it an achievement.

FLORENCE: SIX MONTHS LATER

25. *One of the first days of May.*

An ancient, dilapidated villa crowning an olive-muffled hill.

26. *Through the villa's high, wide doors:*

An overgrown garden, forming a long terrace, with tangles of wild roses and old stone benches, mossy and sun-warmed. Below the parapet of the terrace, the ground drops away steeply to a hazy view of olive trees and vineyards, punctuated by dark strokes of cypresses.

*A litle figure—***Pansy Osmond***—fifteen, in hat and white muslin, moves among old rose bushes in the garden, picking roses.*

Gilbert Osmond—*in his forties, languid, with no clue as to his nationality: "an elegant, complicated medal struck off for a special occasion"—watches his daughter from the shadowy coolness of his rooms.*

Although much about the apartment is shabby, the rooms are of perfect proportions, and the collections of objects, tapestries, paintings, in their subtly studied arrangements, show the taste of an original collector.

Books and journals, magazines and newspapers piled around the room, shabby brocade, stacked paintings, a piano, a little unframed watercolor on an easel, give a slightly bohemian air to the rooms.

OSMOND: She seems to me very *gentille*. She's really pretty.

He turns to two **nuns***—who wait with their businesslike modesty—behind him in the room.*

OSMOND: When her mother died I sent you my daughter to see what you'd make of her. I had faith, you know.

NUN 1: She's perfect. She has no faults.

NUN 2: Of all those we lose this year she's the one we shall miss the most.

NUN 1: We've had her since she was so small.

OSMOND: It's not certain you'll lose her.

NUN 2: Monsieur, good as she is, she's not one of us— she's made for the world.

OSMOND: Nothing's settled yet.

They watch as **Pansy** *hurries across the terrace towards them, carrying two bunches of roses still warm from the garden, one red, one white. A slim, small girl with a "small face painted with a fixed and intensely sweet smile."*

PANSY: It's only the color that's different, Mamman. There are just as many in one bunch as in the other.

Pansy *steps from the hazy dazzle of the terrace into the shadowy interior.*

27. *A horse pulling a carriage, straining up the steepest of hillside roads.*

Inside the carriage is **Madame Merle***, wearing a mantilla.*

———

28. *Madame Merle* crosses the piazza towards the ancient solid mask of Osmond's hilltop villa. A few **loungers** on stone benches under the high shuttered windows.

29. *The* **nuns**, now each holding a bunch of roses, bend to take turns kissing **Pansy's** forehead, as **Osmond** crosses to the door.

30. *A* **footboy** in shabby livery ushers **Madame Merle** across the villa's tiled antechamber, high as a chapel, as:

Osmond opens the door. His slight breath of surprise to see **Madame Merle**.

They do not greet each other, only a second's assessing glance. At the door:

MADAME MERLE: Is there someone here?
OSMOND: Yes. Someone you may see.

31. *Madame Merle*, coming into Osmond's apartment, is confronted by **Pansy**, between the two **nuns**, a hand in the arm of each.

PANSY: Ah, Madame Merle!

Madame Merle holds out both hands:

MADAME MERLE: I have come to welcome you home.

Pansy comes to Madame Merle and presents her forehead to be kissed.

Madame Merle, hands on Pansy's shoulders, keeps the girl with her as the nuns, bowing low to Madame Merle, pass out of the room with Osmond.

PANSY: May I not go to the carriage?
MADAME MERLE: It would please me better if you'd remain with me.

Madame Merle sits and draws Pansy's little hand across her own palm, inspecting it.

MADAME MERLE: I hope they always see that you wear gloves. Little girls usually dislike them.
PANSY: I used to dislike them, but I like them now.
MADAME MERLE: I'll make you a present of a dozen.
PANSY: Will they be very pretty?
MADAME MERLE: Not too pretty.

They have heard the sound of Osmond's steps across the antechamber. Madame Merle releases Pansy and stands. Osmond comes into the room. He doesn't look at Madame Merle. Rather, he rearranges a few chairs as she and Pansy watch.

PANSY: She's going to give me some gloves.

MADAME MERLE: You needn't tell that to everyone, my dear.

OSMOND: You're very kind to her. She's supposed to have everything she needs.

MADAME MERLE: I should think she'd had enough of the nuns.

OSMOND: If we're going to discuss that matter she had better go out of the room.

MADAME MERLE: Let her stay. We'll talk of something else.

OSMOND: Go into the garden, *mignonne*, and pluck a flower or two for Madame Merle.

PANSY: That's just what I want to do.

Osmond follows Pansy to the door. He stands watching her for a moment, then moves back into the room, where he wanders about.

MADAME MERLE: There's something I should like you to do in Florence. There's a friend of mine I want you to know.

OSMOND: What good will that do me?

MADAME MERLE: It will amuse you. If only I could induce you to make an effort.

OSMOND: Ah, there you are. I knew something tiresome was coming. What in the world—that's likely to turn up here—is worth an effort?

MADAME MERLE: The person I came to Florence to see. She's a niece of Mrs. Touchett. She's young—twenty-three years old. I met her in England, six months ago. I like her immensely, and I do what I don't do every day, I admire her. You'll do the same.

OSMOND: Not if I can help it.

MADAME MERLE: You won't be able to help it.

OSMOND: Is she beautiful, clever, rich, splendid, universally intelligent, unprecedentedly virtuous? It's only on those conditions that I care to make her acquaintance. I know plenty of dingy people. I don't want to know any more.

MADAME MERLE: Miss Archer isn't dingy. She fills all your requirements.

OSMOND: More or less, of course.

MADAME MERLE: No, quite literally.

*She waits while **Osmond** turns all this over.*

OSMOND: What do you want to do with her?

MADAME MERLE: What you see. Put her in your way.

OSMOND: Isn't she meant for something better than that?

MADAME MERLE: I don't pretend to know what people are meant for. I only know what I can do with them.

OSMOND: I'm sorry for Miss Archer.

MADAME MERLE: If that's the beginning of interest in her, I take note of it.

*They are now face to face. **Madame Merle** settles her mantilla, looking down at it, watched by **Osmond**.*

OSMOND: You're looking very well. You're never so well as when you've got an idea—they're always becoming to you.

"At a certain moment the element between them, whatever it was, always levelled itself and left them more closely face to face than either ever was with anyone else."

MADAME MERLE: I wish very much you were not so heartless. It has always been against you, and it will be against you now.

OSMOND: I'm not so heartless as you think. Every now and then something touches me, as for instance your ambitions for me. You are, after all, the most remarkable of women. I don't see why you think Mrs. Touchett's niece should matter to me, when—when—

MADAME MERLE: When I myself have mattered so little?

OSMOND: That is not what I meant to say, of course. When I've known and appreciated such a woman as you.

MADAME MERLE: Isabel Archer's better than I.

Osmond gives a small laugh, and the intimate sexuality of the mood changes.

Osmond turns to a little watercolor propped on easel.

OSMOND: Have you seen my latest?

MADAME MERLE: You know I don't care for your drawings.

OSMOND: They're really so much better than other people's.

MADAME MERLE: But as the only thing you do—well, it's so little. I should have liked you to do so many other things. Those were my ambitions.

OSMOND: Things that were impossible.

MADAME MERLE: Things that were impossible.

She looks around his rooms.

MADAME MERLE: Your rooms at least are perfect. You've such adorable taste.

OSMOND: I'm sick of my adorable taste.

MADAME MERLE: You must let Miss Archer come and see it. As *cicerone* of your museum you appear to particular advantage.

Osmond colder, more attentive:

OSMOND: Did you say she was rich?

MADAME MERLE: There's no doubt whatever about her fortune. See her, make a beginning, that's all I ask of you.

OSMOND: A beginning of what?

A little silence between them.

MADAME MERLE: I want you of course to marry her.

32. *Isabel's room at Palazzo Crescentini, open to the sunlit terrace outside.*

Ralph lolls on a sofa—watching Isabel as she moves around, in and out of her bathroom, putting away purchases—in the pleasurable intimacy of their being together again.

ISABEL: Do you think it good for me to be made so rich? Henrietta doesn't.

RALPH: Oh, hang Henrietta! If you ask me I'm delighted at it.

ISABEL: Did you know your father intended to leave me so much money?

RALPH: What does it matter whether I know? My father was very obstinate.

ISABEL: So you did know.

RALPH: Yes, he told me.

ISABEL: How did he know I will make good use of such a large fortune? How did he know I'm not weak?

RALPH: Don't ask yourself so much whether this or that is good for you. Live as you like best, and your character will take care of itself.

Isabel sits, squeezing up beside him, and with a "tender ferocity":

ISABEL: I wonder if you know what you say, If you do you take a great responsibility.

33. *A narrow, angular street, made shadowy by the tall houses rising on either side, is like a "little corridor leading out from the past," an unknown kingdom at the far end. A carriage appears.*

34. *In the carriage **Madame Merle** sits opposite **Isabel**, glancing at her with approval. Sound of horses, the movement of the carriage as it swings around angular bends.*

MADAME MERLE: You look charming. You are never disappointing.

Isabel perversely prickly:

ISABEL: I didn't realize I was under an obligation to charm Mr. Osmond.
MADAME MERLE: My dear child, it's not a question of his liking you. I don't speak for him, poor man.

35. *Isabel steps into the cool shadows of Osmond's antechamber, leaving the bright day behind her.*

36. *Osmond's sister, the **Countess Gemini**——"thin and dark with features that suggest a tropical bird, her fashionable plumage shimmering and elegant, has a great deal of manner."*

She is the only one seated of the little party and is in full flight.

***Isabel, Madame Merle**, and **Pansy** with **Osmond**, who stands awkwardly, smiling and glancing about as his sister talks.*

COUNTESS: I don't come to see my brother, I make him come and see me. This hill of his is impossible. Really, Osmond, you'll be the ruin of my horses. I heard them wheezing today. It's very disagreeable to hear one's horses wheezing. I must tell you that Osmond doesn't often invite me. It was quite my own idea, coming today. I like to see new people, and I'm sure you're very new. But don't sit there, that chair's not what it looks. There are some very good seats here, but there are also some horrors.

As they all find chairs:

ISABEL: I don't see any horrors anywhere. Everything seems to me beautiful and precious.
OSMOND: Thank you. I've a few good things. Indeed, I've nothing very bad.
COUNTESS: Poor Osmond, with his old curtains and crucifixes!
OSMOND: Won't you have some tea? You must be very tired.
ISABEL: No, I'm not tired. What have I done to tire me?

Isabel feels a need to be very direct, to pretend to nothing.

COUNTESS: You'll be tired when you go home, if he shows you all his bibelots and gives you a lecture on each.
ISABEL: If I'm tired I shall have at least learned something.

The Countess Gemini is off again:

COUNTESS: For me, one should like a thing or one shouldn't, but one shouldn't attempt to reason it out. There are some very good feelings that may have very bad reasons. And then there are very bad feelings sometimes that have good reasons. Don't you see what I mean?

*But **Madame Merle** has stood:*

MADAME MERLE: It's too beautiful a day—shall we go into the garden?

*As they all stand, **Madame Merle** takes the **Countess's** arm in hers and leads her out, still talking:*

COUNTESS: I don't care anything about reasons, but I know what I like.

***Osmond** waits for **Isabel** to sit, then sits and reaches out to draw **Pansy** to stand between his knees. She leans against him while he passes his arm around her slimness. **Pansy** gazes at **Isabel**.*

OSMOND: Miss Archer, what do you think of my sister?
ISABEL: Don't ask me that, I've seen your sister too little.
OSMOND: Yes, you've seen her very little, but I should like to know how she strikes a fresh, unprejudiced mind.

***Isabel** goes to look at Osmond's paintings, the soft glow of old tapestries, medieval treasures, artfully arranged.*

OSMOND: I sometimes think we've got into rather a bad way, living here amongst people and things not our own. My sister's rather unhappy, and as she's not of a serious turn she doesn't tend to show it tragically, she shows it comically instead. Let me take that picture down, you want more light.

Osmond reaches up and lifts down the little painting, holding it to the light for Isabel. Pansy looks from face to face as Osmond tells Isabel a few curious details about the painting.

37.   *The shabby footboy has placed two chairs out on the terrace for Madame Merle and the Countess. The narrow, overgrown garden beyond, stretching away to the view.*

COUNTESS: I have to tell you, I don't approve of your plan.

MADAME MERLE: You think me more calculating than I am.

COUNTESS: It's not your calculating I think ill of, it's your calculating wrong. I've seen the girl but this once, and I like her very much.

MADAME MERLE: So do I.

COUNTESS: You've a strange way of showing it.

MADAME MERLE: I advise you not to agitate yourself. The matter concerns three persons much stronger of purpose than yourself.

COUNTESS: Three persons? You and Osmond, of course. But is Miss Archer also very strong?

MADAME MERLE: Quite as much so as we.

COUNTESS: You're capable of anything, you and Osmond. You're dangerous.

MADAME MERLE: You had better leave us alone, then.

COUNTESS: I like her.

MADAME MERLE: I don't think she likes you.

COUNTESS: You *are* dangerous, even by yourself.

MADAME MERLE: If you want her to like you, don't abuse your brother to her. We mustn't forget he is one of the cleverest of men.

COUNTESS: I haven't yet discovered what he has done.

MADAME MERLE: He has known how to wait.

COUNTESS: To wait for Miss Archer's money? Well, it's a pity she's so charming. To be sacrificed, any girl would do.

Osmond and Isabel, while the two women talk, have walked down the terrace through the tangled overgrown garden.

They have come to the balustrade at the far end of the terrace overlooking the view. The late sun makes the hillside golden and the shadows glow purple.

OSMOND: Madame Merle spoke of you having some plan of going round the world.

ISABEL: I'm rather ashamed of my plans. I make a new one every day.

OSMOND: I don't see why you should be ashamed—it's the greatest of pleasures. I made one years ago, and I'm acting on it today.

ISABEL: It must have been a very pleasant one.

OSMOND: It was very simple. It was to be as quiet as possible.

ISABEL: As quiet?

OSMOND: Not to worry, not to strive nor struggle. To resign myself, to be content with little. I've passed a great many years here on that plan. I've not been at all unhappy. The events of my life have been absolutely unperceived by anyone save myself—getting an old silver crucifix at a bargain, or discovering, as I once did, a sketch by Correggio.

ISABEL: That's a very pleasant life, to renounce everything but Correggio.

OSMOND: Perhaps I shall have to change, to do something else. I've no longer myself to think of. My daughter's growing up and may very possibly not care so much for the Correggios and crucifixes. I shall have to do what's best for Pansy.

They turn and start walking back.

ISABEL: She's such a dear little girl.

OSMOND: She's my great happiness! It polishes me up a little to talk to you. But you'll be gone before I see you three times. That's what it is to live in a country people come to. But don't imagine I'm whining about it. It's one's own fault if one isn't happy.

*At the far end of the terrace the **footboy** has carried out more chairs and a little table with tea things to where **Madame Merle** and the **Countess** sit. **Pansy** waits at the table to perform her little tea ceremony.*

38. *The sun strikes enormous sheets of patched and holey canvas, attached from high on buildings down to street, forming a makeshift colonnade. A small breeze makes the canvas billow.*

Under the canvas, the shadowy light is full of moving, reflected colors from the faded blues and tans and ochres of the awnings.

Mrs. Touchett brings her worries to Madame Merle as they stroll, amongst people, down the length of the canvas colonnade. Small children run and play, their footsteps echoing and voices calling.

MRS. TOUCHETT: You know everything, tell me—is that curious creature really making love to my niece?

Madame Merle ponders a moment.

MADAME MERLE: Gilbert Osmond? Heaven help us, that's an idea!

MRS. TOUCHETT: Hadn't it occurred to you?

MADAME MERLE: You make me feel an idiot, but I confess it hadn't. I wonder if it has occurred to Isabel.

MRS. TOUCHETT: I shall ask her.

MADAME MERLE: Don't put it into her head. The thing would be to ask Mr. Osmond.

MRS. TOUCHETT: I can't do that. I won't have him inquire of me, with that air of his, what business it is of mine.

MADAME MERLE: I'll ask him myself.

MRS. TOUCHETT: But what business is it of yours?

MADAME MERLE: Its being none whatever is just why I can afford to speak. I'll investigate and report to you.

MRS. TOUCHETT: He has nothing in the world but a dozen or two early masters and a more or less pert little daughter.

———

39. *A lazy Italian-English afternoon tea party in a large salon off the sunlit terrace of the Palazzo Crescentini. Tea things, newspapers, maps, guidebooks, and so on strewn around our jolly party:* **Henrietta, Bob Bantling, Ralph,** *and* **Isabel,** *who is crossing the room with* **Osmond** *to show him out:*

OSMOND: I should like to be in Ravenna with you.
ISABEL: You might come, then.
OSMOND: But you'll have a lot of people with you.
ISABEL: Of course, I shall not be alone.

40. *A* **Turkish dancer,** *a* **musician,** *and a* **singer** *in the Countess Gemini's palazzo. The singer's voice casts its haunting exotic sound over the fashionable crowded party of mainly Italians, with a few of the international community amongst them.*

Most of the **guests** *are dressed in versions of Turkish costume. Small barefoot Italian* **boy servants,** *also dressed in the party theme, carry around trays of drinks.*

Madame Merle *and* **Osmond** *pass the* **dancer** *and music, walking through the crowded rooms.* **Madame Merle** *elegantly, subtly in costume, while* **Osmond** *wears his usual clothes.*

OSMOND: She wants me to go to Ravenna with her.
MADAME MERLE: To go with her?
OSMOND: To be there while she's there. She proposed it. Of course I gave her a chance.

MADAME MERLE: I rejoice to hear it, but don't cry victory too soon. Of course you'll go.

OSMOND: It makes me work, this idea of yours.

MADAME MERLE: Don't pretend you don't enjoy it.

The two conspirators have seated themselves on a large ottoman: Osmond half beside, half behind Madame Merle, who smiles as she talks, glancing around the room, conscious of not giving an appearance of intimacy.

MADAME MERLE: You've made a very good impression, and I've seen for myself that you've received one. You've not come to Mrs. Touchett's so often to oblige me.

OSMOND: The girl's not disagreeable. She has only one fault.

MADAME MERLE: What's that?

OSMOND: Too many ideas.

MADAME MERLE: I warned you she was clever.

OSMOND: Fortunately they're very bad ones.

MADAME MERLE: Why is that fortunate?

OSMOND: No loss, if they must be sacrificed.

They take drinks from a little servant. A silence as Madame Merle looks out into the room.

MADAME MERLE: You're unfathomable. I'm frightened at the abyss into which I've cast her.

OSMOND: You can't draw back, you've gone too far.

MADAME MERLE: Very good, but you must do the rest yourself.

Two **Italian women** have started to do a Turkish dance, to much encouragement and laughter.

41. A long procession of strange white-robed mosaic figures flows high up, under the roof, along the wall of San Apollinare Nuovo in Ravenna. The gold background glows in the shadowy coolness.

Amongst the shining marble columns a party of **schoolboys** with their **priest-teachers**: the sound of their voices and feet as they move around the chapel.

Ralph, Isabel, Henrietta, and **Bantling** stare up, inspecting the mosaics. **Bantling** jolly and attentive, finding likenesses to people he knows, delighting **Henrietta,** with notebook. **Ralph**'s happiness to be with **Isabel,** to watch the spell of the mosaics on her. He feels blessed to be carrying her parasol.

Isabel, for a moment separated from the others by **schoolboys** and **priests,** continues to move further down the chapel, drawn along by the line of saints.

She pauses and sees:

The back of a familiar head in the pew ahead.

Isabel's breath taken away.

*She walks on and turns and looks down at **Osmond**, who glances at her for a brief second before he stands. After a silence:*

ISABEL: So you decided to come.

OSMOND: I came last night.

ISABEL: The others are here.

OSMOND: I didn't come here for the others. I came to say goodbye. Who knows if you will come back? You're under no obligation to.

ISABEL: You think my travels ridiculous.

OSMOND: No—go everywhere, do everything. Be happy, be triumphant.

As they move further into the darkness:

ISABEL: What do you mean by "triumphant"?

OSMOND: Well, doing what you like.

ISABEL: Doing all the vain things one likes may be tiresome.

OSMOND: Exactly, and you'll be tired someday. I don't know whether I'd better not wait until then for something I want to say to you.

ISABEL (*nervous*): I can't advise you without knowing what it is. But I'm horrid when I'm tired.

OSMOND: I don't believe that. You're angry sometimes, that I can believe. But I'm sure you're never cross.

ISABEL: Not even when I lose my temper?

OSMOND: You don't lose it, you find it, and that must be beautiful.

ISABEL: If only I could find it now.

OSMOND: I'm not afraid. I should fold my arms and admire you.

A long pause between them, before:

OSMOND: What I wish to say is that I find I'm in love with you.
ISABEL: Ah, that had better wait!

Isabel moves away quickly, nervously, but Osmond moves to block her from leaving.

OSMOND: No, you may heed it now or never, as you please, but after all I must say it.

"She had turned away, but in the movement she had stopped herself and dropped her gaze on him. The two remained a while in this situation, exchanging a long look—the large, conscious look of the critical hours of life."

OSMOND: I'm absolutely in love with you.
ISABEL: Oh, don't say that, please.
OSMOND: I haven't the idea that it will matter much to you. I've neither fame nor fortune. So I offer nothing.
ISABEL: I think I'm glad that we're separating.
OSMOND: If you were not going away you'd know me better.
ISABEL: I shall do that some other time.
OSMOND: There's one thing more. There's a little service I should like to ask. I am going to Rome for several days. Go and see my little daughter before you leave Florence.

Ralph, looking down the chapel for Isabel, sees her and then realizes who she is talking with. His alarm as he recognizes the meaning of Osmond's effort in coming to Ravenna.

42.   *On Osmond's hilltop: a little tea table abandoned in shade on terrace.*

Further along: a distinct line between the villa's shadow and the sunlit garden beyond.

Isabel and Pansy walking together.

At the shadow line Pansy stops: a little dancer in second position.

Isabel walks on into the sunlight's dazzle.

Then she stops, turning back to Pansy, stranded beyond the shadow line.

PANSY: Papa says while he is away I am not to go beyond this line.
ISABEL: Your father says that?
PANSY: He says I will get scorched.

Isabel puts up her parasol.

ISABEL: Here you are—share my parasol.

Isabel turns to walk on, but Pansy doesn't follow. Isabel turns back again. Pansy is almost in tears.

ISABEL: What is it?

Pansy bursts into tears. Isabel goes to Pansy, tenderly takes her hand.

ISABEL: No, you're right to do as your father says. He'll never ask you anything unreasonable.

The two turn back towards the villa, walking together in the cool shade, and disappear into the dark interior of Osmond's apartment.

TURKEY

43. *A pervasive tide of sound, advancing and receding, rising and falling: the sound of Islamic prayers chanted by thousands of male voices.*

*On the ramparts of a mosque: a number of **tourists** with **guides**, all nationalities, many languages.*

*Isabel and **Madame Merle** with their French-speaking **Turkish guide**. Isabel head-down reading her Baedeker. **Madame Merle**, weary, fixes a boot, fans herself, tries to block out the endless noise. Their **guide**, ignoring his lack of audience, talks on.*

44. *English luggage—piled up in a village hotel courtyard— being loaded onto camels. Flies cover backs, are waved away from faces.*

*Madame Merle and an English **maid** count off pieces of luggage against a list. The hotel **porters** are arguing with the **guide** and the **maid**, denying any knowledge of the missing cases:*

MAID: —nine, ten, eleven, twelve—you see?—there should be fourteen—*two more*—*two*—two more pieces— (*looks at list*) a second hatbox and—(*to guide*) do they understand?

*But the **porters** are arguing, in Arabic, over her, between themselves. The **maid** could cry as the **guide** joins in.*

***Women** in chadors, only their eyes visible, lean out of windows above, in clusters: a lively commentary on amount of luggage, style of clothes, of these uncovered foreign women.*

***Isabel** very aware of the scrutiny from above. She sneaks a look up at the women, who laugh and duck out of sight. Then a few shyly reappear, staring down again at this rarity.*

45. *Pamukkale: the hypnotic contours of the salt limestone formations. **Isabel** stares at them, her face lit by the light off the salt.*

*Much commotion as **Isabel**, in full-length bathing gear and cap, is lowered in a chair-contraption, behind a decorative screen, into the steamy salt-spring pool.*

***Madame Merle**, listless in a corner of shade under a parasol, sits on a donkey. The English **maid** busy with portable tea things. The **guide** keeps away hawkers and beggars. High noise of many voices. Heat. Flies.*

Sound fainter in the pool.

Isabel, *only her capped head visible, among a few other* **European women**—*also only their heads seen*—*in steamy, rippling water. No one looks at anyone else.*

FLORENCE: ONE YEAR LATER

46. *Early summer morning in a Florence square. A long arcaded colonnade holds shadowy light. In the coolness before the heat of day:* **sweepers** *sweeping steps, and* **people** *out and about at the beginning of the working day. Again,* **Caspar Goodwood** *stands out, with his faster, more purposeful stride. Sound of bells ringing.*

47. *Caspar puts his calling card onto a tray held out by a* **manservant**, *who moves away, leaving* **Caspar** *in Palazzo Crescentini's entrance hall.*

48. *Isabel, in clothes of shimmering splendor, stands with her back to the little salon, hands clasped behind her, holding Caspar's card. She stands in front of tall windows, their partly open shutters letting in a slice of dazzling light and warmth.*

Behind her, the **manservant** *ushers* **Caspar** *into the salon and closes the door.*

Caspar waits, watching **Isabel**, *who is unmoving at the windows for a moment before she turns to him.*

ISABEL: I can't tell you how I hoped you wouldn't come.
CASPAR: I've no doubt of that.
ISABEL: I gave you full warning that I'd do as I choose.

Caspar's *misery and his insistence irritates* **Isabel**, *who is afraid of him and yet ashamed of her fear.*

CASPAR: I wanted to hear what you had to say in explanation of your having changed your mind.
ISABEL: In explanation? Do you think I'm bound to explain?
CASPAR: You were very positive. I did believe it.
ISABEL: So did I.
CASPAR: When I had your letter I thought there might be some mistake.
ISABEL: There's no mistake whatever.
CASPAR: I saw that as soon as I came into the room. Well, I've done what I wished, I've seen you.
ISABEL: Do you mean you came simply to look at me?
CASPAR: I wished to hear the sound of your voice.
ISABEL: You've heard it and it says nothing very sweet.

49. *Mrs.* **Touchett** *inspecting—in her fluent Italian—the cleaning and repair of plaster and paint work on an ancient frescoed wall around a salon doorway.*

Isabel comes straight to the point as her aunt finishes her question-and-answer session with the **artisans**.

ISABEL: Aunt Lydia, I've something to tell you.
MRS. TOUCHETT: You needn't tell me. I know what it is.
ISABEL: I don't know how you know.

As they move into the salon, negotiating the workmen's floor coverings and equipment in the empty room, and out into long, shadowy corridor, criss-crossed with bars of sunlight from a series of open windows:

MRS. TOUCHETT: The same way that I know when the window's open—by feeling a draft. You're going to marry that man.
ISABEL: What man do you mean?
MRS. TOUCHETT: Madame Merle's friend, Mr. Osmond.
ISABEL: I don't know why you call him "Madame Merle's friend." Is that the principal thing he's known by?
MRS. TOUCHETT: If he's not her friend he ought to be, after what she has done for him.
ISABEL: If you mean that Madame Merle has had anything to do with my engagement, you're greatly mistaken.
MRS. TOUCHETT: You mean that your attractions were sufficient, without the gentleman having to be lashed up? You're quite right. They're immense, your attractions, and he would never have presumed to think of you if she hadn't put him up to it. She has deceived me. She had as good as promised me to prevent your marriage.
ISABEL: She couldn't have prevented it.
MRS. TOUCHETT: While I was waiting for her to interfere, you were marching away, and she was really beating the

drum. He has no money, he has no name, he has no importance. I value such things and I have the courage to say it.

ISABEL: I think I value everything that's valuable. I care very much for money, and that's why I wish Mr. Osmond to have a little.

MRS. TOUCHETT: Give it to him then, but marry someone else.

50. *High, densely smooth bushes clipped into rounded cones, like giant stones. **Isabel** walks amongst them: their cool, dark greenness close above and around her. For a moment she pauses—frowning, grave, with a sense of time lost—but she will lose no more, and with this decision made, she hurries out from the grove of bushes and onto the palazzo's sunlit lawn.*

51. *Palazzo Crescentini's stables—huge and blue-painted— where **Ralph** has come to be alone.*

*He watches as **Isabel**, as if bidden out of his thoughts of her, appears in the stable doorway. She comes through the stables to him.*

ISABEL: You didn't come up to lunch.

RALPH: I am not hungry.

ISABEL: You ought to eat. You live on air.

RALPH: I haven't congratulated you.

ISABEL: I wondered why you were silent.

RALPH: I think I've hardly got over my surprise since my mother told me. You were the last person I expected to see caught.

ISABEL: I don't see why you call it "caught."

RALPH: Because you're going to be put in a cage.

ISABEL: If I like my cage, that needn't trouble you.

RALPH: You must have changed immensely. A year ago you valued your liberty beyond everything. You wanted only to see life.

ISABEL: I've seen it. And it doesn't look to me now such an inviting expanse.

RALPH: I had treated myself to a charming vision of your future. I had amused myself with planning out a high destiny for you. There was to be nothing of this sort in it. You were not to come down so easily or so soon.

ISABEL: Come down?

RALPH: It hurts me—hurts me as if I had fallen myself.

Isabel's pain and bewilderment:

ISABEL: I don't understand you.

RALPH: I should have said that the man for you would have had a more active, larger, freer sort of nature. (*He hesitates.*) I can't get over the sense that Osmond is somehow—well, small.

Isabel makes it sound immense:

ISABEL: "Small"?

RALPH: I think he's narrow, selfish. He takes himself so seriously. He's the incarnation of taste.

63

ISABEL: His taste is exquisite.

RALPH: Have you ever seen such a taste—a really exquisite one—ruffled?

ISABEL: I hope I will never fail to gratify my husband's.

RALPH (*suddenly passionate*): Ah, that's willful, that's unworthy of you. You were meant for something better than to keep guard over the sensibilities of a sterile dilettante.

Isabel stands quickly, and so does Ralph.

RALPH: I've said what I had on my mind. I've said it, because I love you.

ISABEL: Then you are not disinterested!

RALPH: I love you, but without hope.

Ralph forces a smile; he has said more than he intended.

Isabel has moved away, looking into the sunny stillness of the courtyard. She turns back. Ralph is pained as she defends her choice.

ISABEL: I see Mr. Osmond in quite another way. He's not important—no, he's not rich, he has no titles nor honors nor property. If that's what you mean when you call him "small," then he's as small as you please. I call that large—it's the largest thing I know. He has the gentlest, kindest, lightest spirit. You've got hold of some false idea. It's a pity, but I can't help it.

RALPH: I told you last year that if you were to get into trouble I should feel terribly sold. That's how I feel today.

ISABEL: Do you think I'm in trouble?

RALPH: One's in trouble, dear Isabel, when one's in error.

Isabel's ardent coldness:

ISABEL: Very well, I shall never complain of my trouble to you.

She turns away from him, and he watches her cross the garden and disappear into the shadowy, vaulted loggia.

Ralph *feels "shocked and humiliated—his calculations had been false and the person in the world in whom he was most interested was lost."*

52. *During the* passagiatta: *open carriages up and down the Cascine, carrying **fashionable people**, some with children and dogs.*

*They are watched by people on either side of the path. Others stroll up and down, chat in clusters and couples, greetings in passing, dogs tucked under arms, some parasols, everyone hatted, murmur of voices, of carriage wheels and horses. The sweet, dramatic voices of a trio of Neapolitan **singers** attract a small crowd.*

Pansy *passes the **singers**, looks back to check that the distance between herself and **Osmond** and **Isabel** is not too far. She walks on, keeping always only a little ahead of the lovers.*

OSMOND: They think I'm in love with your money.
ISABEL: How do you know what they think?
OSMOND: You've not told me they're pleased, and if they had been I should have had some sign of it. But I only

care for one thing—for your not having the shadow of a doubt.

ISABEL: You know I have not, not one shadow.

OSMOND: I never in my life tried to earn a penny, and I ought to be less subject to suspicion than most people one sees grubbing and grabbing. I won't pretend I'm sorry you're rich—I'm delighted.

ISABEL: There have been moments when I should like to go and kneel by my uncle's grave and thank him, that he gave me money enough for both of us.

OSMOND: My dear girl, I can't tell you, it has made me better, loving you.

Pansy has turned and is coming back towards them with "a smile that seems an appeal for approbation."

OSMOND: I'm not a failure, as I used to think. I've succeeded in two things: I'm to marry the woman I adore, and I've brought up my child in the old way. We'll amuse ourselves with making up some little life for her.

Osmond holds out a hand to Pansy, who arrives, smiling, in front of them. She takes his hand and he draws her around to his other side, and he and Isabel and Pansy walk on, part of the crowd.

ROME: THREE YEARS LATER

53. *In a cool twilight autumn sky a flock of swallows forms a dense mass in flight—the mass loosens and spreads as the birds take separate flight, wheeling and turning, as if in radar connection with each other, then in one fluid movement they re-form in to*

their dense, wheeling mass, swooping and soaring over the Roman rooftops.

One of these rooftops belongs to a narrow old Roman house.

Edward Rosier—a young, gentle American who has lived most of his life in Europe—is crossing the street to this house.

54. *C*eiling and walls are a mass of light drapery: the charming, decorative interior of a tent. Glimpses of idyllic pastoral landscapes, people bathing, seen between the drapery.

*When we discover **Rosier** and **Madame Merle** coming into the tent—continuing their conversation—we realize it is an illusion: trompe l'oeil.*

MADAME MERLE: What have you got besides your Spanish lace and Dresden teacups?

ROSIER: My collection's very well thought of, and I've a comfortable little fortune, about forty thousand francs a year. Miss Osmond and I can live beautifully on that.

MADAME MERLE: Beautifully, no, sufficiently, yes. Her father can give you nothing.

ROSIER: He lives like a rich man.

MADAME MERLE: The money's his wife's. She brought him a large fortune.

ROSIER: Mrs. Osmond is very fond of her stepdaughter. She may do something.

MADAME MERLE: For a lovesick man you have your wits

about you. No, she will probably prefer to keep her money for her own children.

ROSIER: Her own children? Surely she has none.

MADAME MERLE: She may have yet. She had a poor little boy, who died almost two years ago.

ROSIER: I am sorry. She's a splendid woman.

MADAME MERLE: I don't say your offer's to be jumped at, but there might be a worse one. Mr. Osmond, however, will incline to believe he can do better.

ROSIER: *He* can do better perhaps, but his daughter can't do better than marry the man she loves. For she does, you know. Meanwhile, I'll say a word to Mrs. Osmond.

MADAME MERLE: No, don't set her going, or you'll spoil everything. Her husband's sure to have other views. I advise you not to multiply points of difference between them. Let the matter alone until I've taken a few soundings.

ROSIER: Let the matter alone? But I'm in love.

MADAME MERLE: You won't burn up.

Madame Merle *strokes one of her three black cats.*

55. *In the very heart of Rome:*

*Through the wide, massively arched loggia of the Palazzo Roccanera—the Palace of the Black Rock—we go inside, where **servants**, carrying laden trays, are coming out of the service rooms. We go with them—their chat in Italian, their laughter, footsteps*

—*up through the palace, the sound of a string quartet tuning up becoming clearer.*

56. $\mathcal{T}$*he* **string quartet** *is tuning up.*

Osmond *looks at them critically, as if at an unsatisfactory painting.*

He interrupts, in Italian, making them—with the help of a **servant** *whom he calls—move their chairs and music stands a few feet to the right, to a perfectly staged position.*

Pansy—*nineteen now—in a blue dress, looking like a little Velásquez Infanta, is checking out the tea-table arrangements with* **another servant**. *In her perfect Italian,* **Pansy** *goes through the tea-making ceremony with the woman.*

Sound of instruments being tuned from another room.

Osmond *strolling down the grand reception rooms, taking in their effect. Money has allowed him to practice his style of cold originality to perfection. Lamps lit, fires burning,* **servants** *arranging glasses, ash trays, other props.*

Masses of flowers. His perfect stage being lit and warmed for guests.

Osmond *pauses by a sofa covered in stiffly arranged cushions and, leaning down, quickly, deftly, rearranges them to look casual, informal, inviting: the master's touch.*

He glances down the vast length of intersecting rooms and sees, at the far end, his wife appear.

*As **Isabel** approaches, closer and closer, we absorb the changes three years have made in her:*

"Slender still, but lovelier than before, she had gained no great maturity of aspect; yet there was an amplitude and brilliancy in her personal arrangements that gave a touch of insolence to her beauty. Her light step drew a mass of drapery behind it; her intelligent head sustained a majesty of ornament. The free, keen girl had become quite another person."

***Osmond** checks his watch.*

OSMOND: Where is Pansy?
ISABEL: She has already come down.

*And indeed, **Pansy** is coming out of the tea room, with her quick, short steps and fixed smile, as eager to please as ever.*

***Osmond** checks his stage, his players: all set.*

He signals the quartet to start playing.

57. *In the now crowded rooms, the music from the quartet mixes with voices, laughter.*

Madame Merle joins Osmond on a small sofa. She watches Rosier's righteously indignant walk as he moves away. She glances about her, allows a few blank-looking pauses: her old habit, in public, to disguise their intimacy.

OSMOND: I hate his proposal. I let him see that. I was rude to him on purpose.

MADAME MERLE: I'll tell him that you'll take time and think it over.

OSMOND: No, don't do that. He'll hang on. I hate talking with a donkey.

MADAME MERLE: He's a gentleman, he has a charming temper, and, after all, a comfortable income.

OSMOND: It's misery, genteel misery—it's not what I've dreamed of for Pansy. This kind of thing doesn't find me unprepared. It's what I educated her for. It was all for this—that when such a case came up she should do what I prefer.

58. *Rosier—insulted by Osmond, full of his sense of injury—has ignored Madame Merle's advice and accosted Isabel:*

ROSIER: Your husband's awfully cold-blooded.

Isabel's inscrutable smile:

ISABEL: You can't expect everyone to be as hot as yourself.

ROSIER: I've never been treated so. What is there against

me? That's not the way I'm usually considered. I could have married twenty times.

ISABEL: It's a pity you didn't. I don't mean twenty times, but once, comfortably. You're not rich enough for Pansy.

ROSIER: She doesn't care a straw for one's money.

ISABEL: No, but her father does.

Rosier looks around at the riches Isabel's money has bought.

ROSIER: Yes, he has proved that.

Isabel quickly moves away, but he follows and catches up with her.

ROSIER: You're offended, and now you'll never help me.

Isabel silent, then almost passionate; her mask drops for a brief moment:

ISABEL: It's not that I won't—I simply can't!

59. *Pansy in charge of tea-making in an adjoining room. Rosier sits on an ottoman beside her tea table, in despair at losing his perfect little jeune fille.*

ROSIER: Do you know what your father said to me just now?

PANSY: Don't speak so loud, everyone will hear.

ROSIER: He says that you have forgotten me.

PANSY: No, I don't forget.

72

ROSIER: Then everything's just the same?

PANSY: Not the very same—Papa has been terribly severe. He forbids me to marry you.

ROSIER: Need you mind that?

PANSY: I can't disobey Papa.

ROSIER: Do you sacrifice me like that?

Pansy lifts the teapot lid and "drops her words in to the pot's aromatic depths":

PANSY: I love you just as much.

ROSIER: What good will that do me?

PANSY: Please don't talk anymore. Papa said I was not to talk with you.

ROSIER: Ah, it's too much!

Rosier groans and drops his head into his hands, staring down at the carpet.

60. *Isabel, with her serene mask, is the perfect hostess, moving from group to group until—startled, changing color—she sees, down the room, Osmond escorting Lord Warburton, negotiating the groups, towards her.*

OSMOND: Isabel, I bring you an old friend.

ISABEL: Lord Warburton.

Isabel hardly knows if she feels pleasure or pain. Neither she nor Warburton is perfectly confident.

73

WARBURTON: I've only just arrived, this evening. I knew you were "at home" on Thursdays, so I came.

OSMOND: You see, the fame of your Thursdays has spread to England.

ISABEL: We're greatly flattered. I've heard of you from time to time.

As Osmond moves away, Warburton turns to Isabel with the "deeper, deepest consciousness of his look, which gradually becomes more serious."

WARBURTON: I'm really very glad to see you. There's something I must tell you without more delay. I've brought Ralph Touchett with me.

Isabel very surprised:

ISABEL: Brought him with you?

WARBURTON: He's at the hotel. He was too tired to come out.

ISABEL: But why has he come to Rome?

WARBURTON: Because he's very far gone, Mrs. Osmond. He can't keep warm, and the further south we come the more he feels the cold. If you don't mind my saying so, I think it was a most extraordinary time for Mrs. Touchett to decide on going to America.

ISABEL: My aunt goes at fixed periods. When the date comes round she starts. She'd have started if Ralph had been dying.

WARBURTON: I sometimes think he is dying.

ISABEL: I'll go to him now!

Warburton a little disconcerted.

WARBURTON: No, not now, he has gone to bed. Go to him in the morning.

Warburton watches Isabel accept this, and they move on, passing through to the tea room.

ISABEL: Very well, in the morning.

Isabel again the hostess, smiling, looking around:

ISABEL: May I introduce you to some of these people?
WARBURTON: Oh, please don't. Unless it be to that young lady in the blue dress. She has a charming face.

Isabel follows Warburton's gaze: Pansy at the tea table, passing cups to servant, a despondent Rosier beside her.

ISABEL: The one at the tea table? That's my husband's daughter.
WARBURTON: Lucky man, your husband. What a dear little maid.
ISABEL: You must meet her.
WARBURTON: In a moment. I like looking at her from here.

He turns to a sofa, waits for Isabel to sit, then joins her. But he does not look again at Pansy.

WARBURTON: Do you know that you've changed, a little?
ISABEL: Yes, a good deal.

WARBURTON: I don't mean for the worse, of course—
and yet how can I say for the better?

61. *A few weeks later, in **Ralph**'s apartment in the Hotel de Paris.*

*Warburton maneuvers **Ralph**'s chair into a patch of autumn sunlight as **Isabel** pushes a footstool in front of the chair. A fire is burning. **Ralph**'s English **manservant** is in and out of the room.*

*Ralph watches **Isabel**: "Something fixed and mechanical in the serenity painted on her mask. He had played the wrong card, and now he had lost the game. He should see nothing, he should learn nothing; for him she would always wear a mask."*

*As **Warburton** helps him back to chair:*

RALPH: I think, after all, you know, that I shan't go to Sicily.
WARBURTON: Won't go to Sicily?
ISABEL: Where will you go?
RALPH: Well, I guess I won't go anywhere.
ISABEL: Do you mean return to England?
RALPH: Oh dear no, I'll stay in Rome.
WARBURTON: Rome won't do for you.
ISABEL: Rome's too cold.
RALPH: It will have to do. I'll make it do. See how well I've been since I arrived.

They look at him: a dying man.

WARBURTON: I recommend you to try Sicily.
RALPH: I can't try. I've done trying. I can't move further.
I can't face that journey. And I haven't a single cousin in
Sicily.
ISABEL: But what does the doctor say?
RALPH: I haven't asked him, and I don't care a fig. If I
die here you will bury me.
ISABEL: You shan't die here.

62. *Isabel comes out of the hotel and crosses the courtyard.*

63. *From the balcony windows above,* **Ralph** *watches* **Isabel**
cross the courtyard.

For **Ralph,** *"the free keen girl had become quite another person;
what he saw was the fine lady who was supposed to represent
something. What did* **Isabel** *represent?"*

Ralph *mutters to himself:*

RALPH: It's Osmond!

As **Isabel** *disappears, and* **Ralph** *turns back into the room, where*
Warburton *lights a cigarette and* **Ralph** *drapes a blanket over his
shoulders:*

WARBURTON: I say, tell me this, did you really mean to go to Sicily when we started?
RALPH: Let me put a question first. Did you come with me quite—platonically?
WARBURTON: I don't know what you mean by that. I wanted to come abroad.
RALPH: I suspect we've each been playing our little game.

A pause, then abruptly:

WARBURTON: I recommend you to get the doctor's consent, all the same.

And **Warburton** *helps* **Ralph** *back to his chair.*

RALPH: The doctor's consent will spoil it.
WARBURTON: You're sacrificing your health to your curiosity, then?
RALPH: I'm not much interested in my health, and I'm deeply interested in Mrs. Osmond.
WARBURTON: So am I. (*Adds quickly*) But not as I once was.
RALPH: Permit me to ask whether it's to bring out *that* fact that you're so very civil to the little girl?
WARBURTON: Does that strike you as ridiculous? Of course there's the difference in our ages—more than twenty years.
RALPH: My dear Warburton, are you serious?
WARBURTON: Perfectly serious, as far as I've got.
RALPH: I'm very glad. And heaven help us, how cheered up old Osmond will be!

WARBURTON: I say, don't spoil it. Do you judge she'll be pleased?

RALPH: The girl? Delighted, surely.

WARBURTON: No, no. I mean Mrs. Osmond.

Ralph, disturbed, draws his blanket more tightly around himself.

64. *Osmond, having been out, is taking off his cloak as he moves down the grand reception rooms towards* **Isabel**. *Around them servants clear and tidy the rooms after one of* **Isabel**'s *"Thursdays."*

Osmond throws down his cloak, which is spirited away by a servant.

OSMOND: Lord Warburton was here?

ISABEL: Yes, he stayed half an hour.

OSMOND: Did he talk to Pansy?

ISABEL: He talked almost only to her.

OSMOND: It seems to me he's attentive. Isn't that what you call it?

ISABEL: I don't call it anything. I've waited for you to give it a name.

OSMOND: That's a consideration you don't always show.

ISABEL: I've determined, this time, to try and act as you'd like.

———

Osmond turns slowly to look at her.

OSMOND: Are you trying to quarrel with me?

ISABEL: No, I'm trying to live at peace.

OSMOND: That's an excellent resolve. Your temper isn't good. That's partly why I've not spoken to you about this business of my daughter's. I was afraid I should encounter opposition. I've sent little Rosier about his business.

Osmond pauses.

OSMOND: You see, I believe my daughter only has to sit perfectly quiet to become Lady Warburton.

ISABEL: Should you like that?

OSMOND: I should like it extremely.

ISABEL: Perhaps she won't sit perfectly still. If she loses Mr. Rosier she may jump up.

OSMOND: Pansy would like to be a great lady. She wishes above all to please.

ISABEL: To please Mr. Rosier, perhaps.

OSMOND: No, to please me. Meantime, I should like our distinguished visitor to speak.

ISABEL: He has spoken—to me. He told me it would be a great pleasure to believe she could care for him.

Osmond turns his head quickly to look at her. For a moment he says nothing; then, sharply:

OSMOND: Why didn't you tell me that?

ISABEL: There was no opportunity. You know how we live.

OSMOND: Why doesn't he speak to me, then?

ISABEL: You should have patience. You know Englishmen are shy.

OSMOND: This one's not. He was not when he made love to you.

Isabel finds this disagreeable.

ISABEL: I beg your pardon. He was extremely so.

Osmond pauses.

OSMOND: You must have a great deal of influence with him. The moment you really wish it you can bring him to the point.

This is more offensive to Isabel.

OSMOND: Well, it lies in your hands. I shall leave it there. With a little goodwill you may manage it. Think that over, and remember how much I count on you.

Again he waits; again she doesn't answer. He strolls from the room.

65. *A seemingly endless corridor, lit at intervals by candles on wall brackets. The candles cast two lines of glowing reflections down onto either side of the corridor's floor.*

Isabel, carrying her candle, walks down the corridor, in the center path between the two lines of glowing reflections, towards the darkness at the far end. "It was the house of darkness, the house of dumbness, the house of suffocation."

66. *A great ball.*

*The **dancers** form a rhythmic pattern on the dance floor. Sound of an orchestra, of talk, laughter, of dancers' feet and rustling, swirling skirts.*

***Pansy**'s vaporous skirts among the dancers. Many of the men in uniform.*

*On the sidelines, lovesick **Rosier** watches his little sweetheart.*

*Then, looking into the crowd beyond the dance floor, he sees **Isabel** and starts to make his way towards her.*

***Isabel**, holding a little bouquet of pansies, watches **Rosier**, with a look of almost military resolution, approach her through the crowd.*

*He gives **Isabel** a fierce look to show he is dangerous, then sees the bouquet and softens.*

ROSIER: It's all pansies—it must be hers.
ISABEL: Yes, it's hers. She gave it to me to hold.
ROSIER: May I hold it a little?

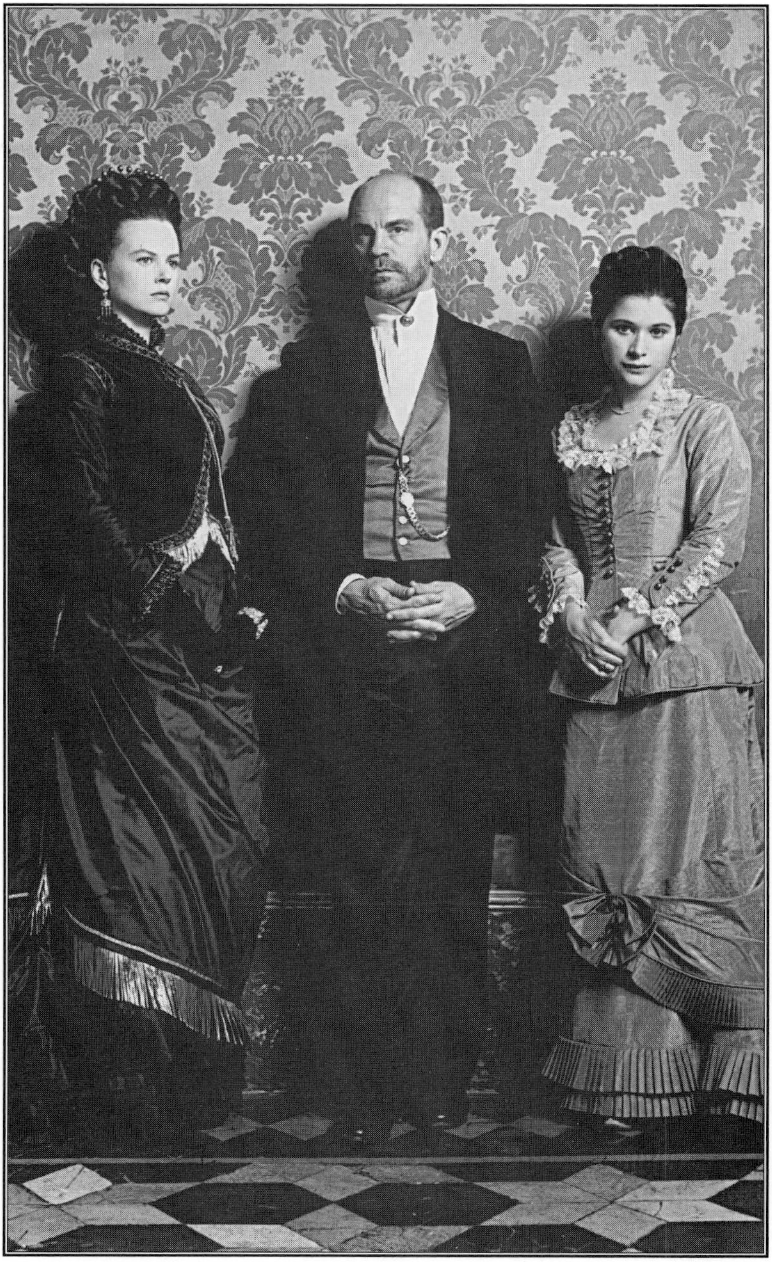

Juergen Teller

Previous Page:
Isabel Archer
(Nicole Kidman),
Gilbert Osmond
(John Malkovich),
and Pansy Osmond
(Valentina Cervi)

Juergen Teller

Pansy Osmond
(Valentina Cervi)

Juergen Teller

Countess Gemini
(Shelley Duvall)

Juergen Teller

Mrs. Touchett
(Shelley Winters)

Juergen Teller

Mr. Touchett
(John Gielgud)

Juergen Teller

Lord Warburton
(Richard E. Grant)

Grant Matthews

Edward Rosier
(Christian Bale)

Juergen Teller

Gilbert Osmond
(John Malkovich)

Grant Matthews

Isabel Archer
(Nicole Kidman)

*Isabel Archer
and
Gilbert Osmond*
(Nicole Kidman
and
John Malkovich)

Ralph Touchett
(Martin Donovan)

Juergen Teller

Madame Merle
(Barbara Hershey)

Juergen Teller

Henrietta Stackpole
(Mary-Louise Parker)

*The Colosseum
in Rome*

Jane Campion

Isabel hesitates.

ROSIER: May I at least have a flower?

Isabel holds out the bouquet:

ISABEL: It's frightful what I'm doing for you.

His glass in one eye, he removes a pansy.

ISABEL: Don't put it in your buttonhole, don't for the
world.
ROSIER: You pity me, but don't you pity her a little?

She is suddenly touched by him.

The set finished, **Pansy**—*escorted by her* **partner**—*moves through
the crowd towards* **Isabel**. *She sees* **Rosier** *is with her stepmother.
He looks at her—a heartfelt, proud look—then turns and walks
away, head up.*

Pansy *counts the flowers in her bouquet.* **Isabel**, *watching, understands this is a sign between the two lovers.*

The next dance now in progress. **Lord Warburton** *has joined*
Isabel *on the sidelines.* **Pansy** *among the dancers with* **another
partner**.

WARBURTON: She has promised to dance with me later.
ISABEL: I suppose you've engaged her for the cotillion.
WARBURTON: No, I didn't ask her for that. It's a qua-
drille.

ISABEL: You're not clever. I told her to keep the cotillion in case you should ask for it.

Warburton laughs frankly.

WARBURTON: Poor little maid, fancy that. She didn't say. Of course I will if you like.
ISABEL: If I like? Oh, if you dance with her only because I like it—!
WARBURTON: I'm afraid I bore her. She seems to have a lot of young fellows on her book.

Isabel rapidly reflects:

ISABEL: Please let me understand.
WARBURTON: Understand what?
ISABEL: You told me ten days ago that you'd like to marry my stepdaughter. You've not forgotten it?
WARBURTON: Forgotten it? I wrote to Mr. Osmond this morning.
ISABEL: He didn't mention to me that he had heard from you.
WARBURTON: I—I didn't send it. It's an awkward sort of letter to write, you know. But I shall send it tonight.
ISABEL: At three o'clock in the morning?
WARBURTON: I mean later, in the course of the day.
ISABEL: Don't forget to send it.
WARBURTON: About the cotillion, the fact is I thought that you—that you—
ISABEL: That I would do it with you? I told you I'd do nothing.

WARBURTON: Exactly. So while it's going on I might find some quiet corner where we may sit and talk.

Rosier leaning, arms folded, in a doorway of the ballroom.

Isabel, followed at a small distance by Warburton, pauses beside Rosier.

ISABEL: Are you not dancing?
ROSIER: Certainly not, if I can't dance with her.
ISABEL: You had better leave, then.
ROSIER: Not until she does.

Rosier won't glance at Warburton as he follows Isabel through the door, past Rosier.

67.   *In an opulent anteroom, where music from the ballroom is fainter, its richness softened by distance, a card game is in progress, servants carry around drinks; little groups of people and couples take time out from the dance floor.*

As Isabel and Warburton look for a quiet corner:

WARBURTON: Who is your dismal friend? I've seen him somewhere before.
ISABEL: It's the young man I've told you about, who's in love with Pansy.
WARBURTON: Ah yes, I remember. He has a face a yard long.

ISABEL: He has reason. My husband won't listen to him.

WARBURTON: Dear me, he looked a well-set-up young fellow.

They have found a sofa and are sitting:

ISABEL: You've a kind thought even for a rival.

Warburton turns quickly, staring at her.

WARBURTON: A rival? You don't mean that she cares for him?

ISABEL: Well, yes, I think she does.

WARBURTON: You told me that she would have no wish apart from her father's, and that he favored me—don't you see—?

ISABEL: I told you that she had an immense wish to please her father.

WARBURTON: That seems to me very proper.

ISABEL: Very proper. But hardly the sort of feeling a man would wish to be indebted for a wife.

A silence as Warburton leans back, staring ahead.

Then he turns to Isabel:

WARBURTON: Why are you so unwilling? So skeptical?

ISABEL: I think Pansy would do wonderfully well to marry you, but you're not really in love.

WARBURTON: Really in love! I won't pretend I'm as I once was.

They look straight at each other and "in that brief, extremely personal gaze, deeper meanings pass between them, that neither is yet fully conscious of."

68. *A carriage passes through the throng of waiting drivers with their carriages and horses outside the embassy.*

Isabel *and* **Pansy,** *both in cloaks, sit next to each other. Their carriage through alternating pools of light and dark as they pass under gas lamps.*

Pansy, *holding her little bouquet, sits back in one corner with an air of fatigue.* **Isabel** *steals a glance at her: the little pale face turned towards the window allows* **Isabel** *to look for a moment longer, as if she can look into the girl's soul to discover what she truly feels.* **Pansy** *lifts her little bouquet and bends her face to its perfumed softness.*

69. *The morning after the ball.* **Isabel** *has come to* **Ralph** *in the Hotel de Paris. Signs of his longer stay: books, journals, papers. Colder now, he has to layer on more clothes.*

ISABEL: I want you to answer me a question. It's about Lord Warburton. Is he really in love?

Ralph's *air of private amusement:*

RALPH: Very much, I think. I can make that out.

ISABEL (*dry*): Ah.

RALPH: You say that as if you were disappointed.

ISABEL: No, only mistaken. I thought I had made out that he doesn't really care for Pansy.

RALPH: For Pansy, no.

ISABEL: But you said just now he did.

Ralph pauses.

RALPH: That he cared for you.

ISABEL: That's nonsense, you know.

RALPH: To me, he has denied it.

Isabel smooths her long gloves, over and over, head down; then looks up, abrupt, passionate.

ISABEL: Ralph, you give me no help!

Ralph shaken by the words' violence.

Isabel's mask gone.

Ralph gives a long murmur of relief, of pity, of tenderness. He feels the gulf between them bridged.

RALPH: How unhappy you must be.

In an instant Isabel's mask is back on. She pretends not to have heard, to Ralph's infinite disappointment.

Both stand.

ISABEL: When I talk of your helping me I talk great nonsense. The idea of troubling you with my domestic embarrassments! Lord Warburton must get on by himself.

*Ralph's desire to have **Isabel** complain of **Osmond**, of seeing her mask drop again, of seeing her natural face.*

RALPH: Your husband may think you haven't pushed enough.
ISABEL: It's a matter we can hardly quarrel about, for almost all the interest is on his side.

She puts out her hand to wish him goodbye.

RALPH: Do you know what his interest will make him say?

He has taken her hand.

RALPH: It will make him say that your lack of zeal is owing to jealousy.

*He pauses, afraid of **Isabel**'s face.*

ISABEL: To jealousy?
RALPH: To jealousy of his daughter.

Her voice one he has never heard before:

ISABEL: You're not kind.

She tries to pull her hand away, but he holds on to it.

89

RALPH: Be frank with me and you'll see.

Isabel pulls harder. He tries to hold on, but she frees her hand and turns and hurries from the room.

Ralph's misery: "He had caught a glimpse of her natural face and he wished immensely to look into it."

He goes to balcony windows to watch her walk across the courtyard. Late autumn frost on morning windows.

70. *Autumn sunshine in the piazza outside Palazzo Roccanera. Morning street life.*

*Isabel, returning from her visit to **Ralph**, gets out of the carriage.*

She walks towards the entrance of Palazzo Roccanera. The warmth of the sun on her back. She pauses, looking up at her prison with its massive, dark, silent presence, taking its measure. Innocent street sounds behind her.

A moment's fear shivers through her body. She has an urge to turn and walk away. But instead, resisting every step, she walks towards the fortress and disappears inside.

71. *Pansy like a "childish victim decked out for sacrifice," tiny in the immense space of her room, with its dark, heavily timbered ceiling. A fire burning; **Isabel** in a chair with **Pansy** on a cushion at her feet, turned to **Isabel**, hands clasped on her stepmother's lap. Both dressed for dinner.*

*In the face of **Pansy**'s shy sincerity **Isabel** has to hide her bitterness and anger.*

ISABEL: If I try to learn what you want, it's only that I may act accordingly.
PANSY: The only thing I want in life is to marry Mr. Rosier.
ISABEL: You must think of something else.
PANSY: You think of those who think of you. I know Mr. Rosier thinks of me.

*Isabel is grateful for the dimness of the room. She feels hideously insincere: it is what she has to do for **Osmond**.*

ISABEL: Your father would like you to make a better marriage.
PANSY: What should you like me to do?

The question is a terrible one.

ISABEL: Lord Warburton has shown you great attention.
PANSY: If you mean that he'll propose for me, I think you're mistaken.
ISABEL: Your father would like it extremely.

Pansy's wise little smile.

PANSY: Lord Warburton won't propose simply to please Papa.

Pansy stands, smiling, "as if in possession of a bright assurance."

PANSY: Oh, no, there's no danger—no danger! It's as if he said to me, "I like you very much, but if it doesn't please you I'll never say it again." And he doesn't care for me either. No, there's no danger.

*Isabel touched with wonder at the depths of **Pansy**'s perception.*

As they cross the room together:

ISABEL: You must tell your father that.
PANSY: I'd rather not.
ISABEL: You oughtn't to let him have false hopes.
PANSY: But it will be good for me that he should. Then Papa won't propose anyone else. And that will be an advantage for me.

*Isabel astounded by **Pansy**'s strength and lucidity. She feels relieved of a heavy responsibility.*

*Pansy holds back heavy curtain over door, for **Isabel** to pass through. **Isabel**'s tender touch to **Pansy**'s face as she passes the girl. **Pansy** follows, letting the curtain fall back into place.*

———

72. *Early evening of another day.* **Osmond** *watches* **Isabel** *move around her sitting room, collecting together a few books. Although he finds it disagreeable to betray his state of expectancy, he quizzes* **Isabel.**

OSMOND: Does Warburton form his words with such difficulty? When he told you he intended to write, what did you say to him?

Isabel, carrying books, moves out of her sitting room. **Osmond** *is forced to follow:*

ISABEL: I think I told him not to forget it.

They move together down the long hallway.

OSMOND: Apparently he has forgotten. Be so good as to remind him.
ISABEL: If you really wish hands to be laid on Lord Warburton, you must lay them yourself.

At the top of the staircase, **Osmond** *pauses:*

OSMOND: That won't be easy, with you working against me.
ISABEL: I told you I would do what I could.
OSMOND: Yes, that gained you time.

Isabel's fear as **Osmond's** *enmity comes out into the open.*

She sees, below them, **Lord Warburton** *being ushered across the entrance hall.*

Osmond follows her gaze.

*Lord Warburton looks up as **Osmond** and **Isabel** come down the staircase.*

ISABEL: My husband and I were just now talking of you.
OSMOND: We wondered what had become of you. We thought that perhaps you had gone away.

*Warburton looks rapidly from **Osmond** to **Isabel**, sensing the tension between them and **Osmond**'s embarrassment.*

WARBURTON: No, I'm only on the point of going.

*They move into a salon, where **Warburton** sits on a small chair, as if only for a moment, hat still in hand.*

WARBURTON: I find myself suddenly recalled to England. I'm awfully sorry to leave poor Touchett.

*For a moment no one speaks. **Isabel** doesn't look at her husband.*

OSMOND (*light*): Take poor Touchett with you.
WARBURTON: He had better wait for warmer weather. I shouldn't advise him to travel just now.

Osmond's air of indifference——"He gave no sign——not the faintest or subtlest——of his inner rage" as:

WARBURTON: Why shouldn't you all come to England? Come and spend a month at Lockleigh. It will amuse

Miss Osmond no end, I am sure. No, you must think seriously about it.

Osmond stands. Isabel almost sorry for him.

OSMOND: I've a letter to write before dinner, you must excuse me. Of course when you come to Rome you'll always look us up.

Osmond gives only a nod, not a handshake, and leaves.

Warburton is awkward with Isabel.

ISABEL: I'm glad it's the last time.
WARBURTON: So am I. She doesn't care for me.
ISABEL: No, she doesn't care for you.

73. *Much later that night, in the grand entrance hall of Palazzo Roccanera, Isabel and Osmond come in with Pansy, all wearing cloaks, bringing cold air in with them. Servants closing doors, taking cloaks.*

Isabel watches as Pansy embraces her father goodnight and Osmond returns her embrace with even more tenderness than usual.

As Pansy turns to go upstairs, Isabel goes to follow her.

OSMOND: Don't go. I have something to say to you.

74. *The fire out, and only a few lights in the great drawing room. Isabel draws her cloak around herself, mortally cold.*

OSMOND: I don't understand what you wish to do.
ISABEL: I wish to go to bed. I'm very tired.

Osmond has arranged a pile of cushions on a vast divan, but Isabel has dropped into an armchair.

OSMOND: I think you're trying to humiliate me. You've played a very deep game. You've managed it beautifully.
ISABEL: What is it that I've managed?
OSMOND: You have kept this whole matter quite in your own hands.

"He was going down, down: the vision of such a fall made her almost giddy. The working of his morbid passion was extraordinary."

ISABEL: Will you tell me in the plainest words of what it is you accuse me?
OSMOND: Of having prevented Pansy's marriage to Warburton. Are those words plain enough?
ISABEL: On the contrary, I took a great interest in it. When you told me you counted on me I accepted the obligation. I was a fool to do so, but I did it.
OSMOND: You pretended to do it. Where is the letter you told me he had written?
ISABEL: I haven't the least idea.
OSMOND: No, you destroyed it.

Isabel stares, a long murmur:

ISABEL: Oh, Gilbert, for a man who was so fine . . . !

OSMOND: I was never so fine as you. You've done everything you wanted. You've got him out of the way without appearing to do so, and you've placed me in the position in which you wished to see me—that of a man who has tried to marry his daughter to a lord, but has grotesquely failed.

ISABEL: Pansy doesn't care for him.

OSMOND: That has nothing to do with the matter.

ISABEL: And he doesn't care for Pansy.

OSMOND: That won't do, you told me he did.

ISABEL: After this, you must attend to such things yourself.

Isabel has stood and taken a candle. Osmond waits a moment.

OSMOND: I thought you were very fond of my daughter.

ISABEL: I've never been more so than now.

OSMOND: Your affection has immense limitations. However, that perhaps is natural.

ISABEL: Is that all you wished to say to me?

OSMOND: Are you satisfied? Am I sufficiently disappointed?

ISABEL: I don't think on the whole you're disappointed. You've had another opportunity to try to stupefy me.

OSMOND: It's not that. It's proved that Pansy can aim high.

ISABEL: Poor little Pansy!

And she leaves with her candle.

75. *A few weeks later in the Hotel de Paris, two Italian nurs-ing nuns set up lamp treatment in* **Ralph***'s sitting room.*

Ralph lies on a sofa; **Henrietta** *sits in a chair beside him.* **Hen-rietta** *"is as keen and quick and fresh as ever, and as neat and bright and fair."*

HENRIETTA: I suppose you know you can't go back to England alone?

RALPH: I have no idea of doing that. I shall have people with me.

HENRIETTA: What do you mean by "people"? Servants whom you pay?

As they talk, **Caspar Goodwood** *comes into the room—familiar with it—bringing the morning newspapers and some mail for* **Ralph***.*

He sits moodily and half-listens to **Ralph** *and* **Henrietta***:*

RALPH: After all, they're human beings.

HENRIETTA: You must have a woman's care.

RALPH: I've had so much of yours for the past fortnight that it will last me a good while.

HENRIETTA: I guess I'll go with you.

Ralph slowly props himself up on the sofa.

RALPH: Go with me?

HENRIETTA: Yes, I know you don't like me, but I'll go with you all the same. It would be better to lie down again.

Ralph looks at her for a while, then lies down.

RALPH: I like you very much.

Henrietta gives one of her infrequent laughs.

HENRIETTA: You needn't think you can buy me off. I'll
go with you, and what is more, I'll take care of you.

*The **nursing nuns** are waiting for **Ralph** to begin treatment: lamps
at the ready, cap and mask. As **Caspar** helps **Ralph** up from the
sofa:*

CASPAR: I'm afraid I shall be a fifth wheel to the coach.
Mrs. Osmond wants me to travel with you, but that isn't
the principal thing. She wants me to leave Rome.
HENRIETTA: She wants us all to leave Rome!

76. *Isabel and **Henrietta** in a room above the Palazzo Roccanera's courtyard.*

*The **Countess Gemini** has arrived from Florence: her carriage is
piled with luggage.*

HENRIETTA: I don't know what you want to do.
ISABEL: I want to be alone.
HENRIETTA: You won't be alone so long as you've so
much company at home.

*They look down to the **Countess** supervising the unloading of her luggage.*

ISABEL: They're part of the comedy. You others are spectators.

HENRIETTA: Do you call it a comedy, Isabel Archer?

ISABEL: Tragedy then, if you like. You're all looking at me. It makes me uncomfortable.

HENRIETTA: You're like the stricken deer seeking the innermost shade. It's too much, having come on purpose, to leave you just as I find you.

77. *C*aspar **Goodwood** *supervising the loading of luggage into a coach, with **Ralph's** manservant and hotel porter.*

***Caspar** sees **Isabel** coming into the courtyard and crosses to meet her.*

***Isabel's** smile fixed and a trifle forced:*

ISABEL: It's wonderfully good of you. I can't tell you how kind I think you.

CASPAR: With a few words like that you make me go.

ISABEL: You must come back someday.

CASPAR: I don't care a straw for your cousin.

ISABEL: Is that what you wished to tell me?

CASPAR: No, no, I didn't want to tell you anything. I can't understand— What am I to believe? What do you want me to think?

Isabel says nothing, but no longer pretends to ease.

CASPAR: If you're unhappy, I should like to know it. That would be something for me. But you yourself say you're happy, and you're somehow so still, so smooth, so hard. You're completely changed. You conceal everything. I haven't really come near you.

ISABEL (*warning*): You come very near.

And she turns and hurries across the courtyard.

Caspar watches her disappear: "he was hopeless, helpless, useless."

78. *Ralph's room cleared of his belongings. Ralph, dressed for his journey, stands with the last of his luggage, ready to be taken down. Medical paraphernalia stacked on a table.*

Isabel has come to say goodbye.

RALPH: You seem uncommonly glad to get rid of us all.

She puts a hand on his arm:

ISABEL: My dear Ralph—!

RALPH: I've seen less of you than I might, but it's been better than nothing. And then I've heard a great deal about you.

ISABEL: I don't know from whom, leading the life you've done.

RALPH: From the voices of the air. Oh, from no one else. I never let other people speak of you. They always say you're "charming," and that's so flat.

They stand face to face, both her hands in his.

ISABEL: You've been my best friend.
RALPH: It was for you that I wanted to live. But I'm of no use to you.

Isabel realizes that she may never see him again. She can't part with him like this.

ISABEL: If you should send for me, I'd come.
RALPH: Your husband won't consent to that.
ISABEL: No, he wouldn't like it. But I might go all the same.
RALPH: I shall keep that for my last pleasure.

Isabel kisses Ralph.

The porter and Ralph's manservant arrive for his luggage.

79. *In the gardens of the Villa Medici:*

A dusky wood of gnarled and twisted little miniature trunks of oaks, with its "dim light as of a fabled, haunted place."

A long mossy staircase climbs the steep slope, gnarled trees on either side, to an unseen destination.

Isabel and Madame Merle appear on the stairs, climbing up. "A dangerous quickness in Madame Merle and an air of irritation which not even her habit of ease is able to hide."

MADAME MERLE: I hoped to find Lord Warburton here, and to be able to congratulate Pansy.

ISABEL: You shouldn't have gone to Naples, then. You should have stayed here to watch the affair.

MADAME MERLE: Do you think it's too late?

ISABEL: It's all over, please let it rest. I've no doubt Osmond will be happy to discuss it with you.

MADAME MERLE: I know what he thinks. He came to see me last evening.

Isabel discomposed but determined to be good-humored:

ISABEL: As soon as you arrived? Then you know all about it.

They have reached the top of the staircase, opening out onto an open, roofed gallery overlooking the autumn gardens. A few little chairs scattered around at base of huge statue.

MADAME MERLE: Your husband judges you severely.

Isabel, choked with bitterness, turns to leave:

ISABEL: Should you like to know how I judge him?

MADAME MERLE: No, because you'd never tell me. Stay, please.

Madame Merle sits on one of the little chairs. Isabel hesitates, then sits. Leaves thick on the ground around them.

MADAME MERLE: I want if possible to learn the truth.

ISABEL: What truth do you speak of?

MADAME MERLE: Just this: whether Lord Warburton changed his mind quite of his own accord or because you recommended it. To please himself, I mean, or to please you. Now don't be unreasonable, don't take offense. If Lord Warburton simply got tired of the poor child, that's one thing, and it's a pity. If he gave her up to please you, it's another. If that's the case, let him off, let us have him!

Isabel horrified: the strange truth, that Madame Merle's interest is identical to Osmond's.

ISABEL: Who are you—what are you?

MADAME MERLE: Ah, you take it like that.

Madame Merle stands.

ISABEL: What have you to do with me?

Isabel looks up at Madame Merle. Isabel's "face was almost a prayer to be enlightened. But the light of this woman's eyes seemed only a darkness."

MADAME MERLE: Everything.

80. *Later that afternoon in the country outside Rome.*

Isabel's carriage and **driver** *wait by the roadside.*

Isabel's tiny figure in the distance, in the glowing blues and purples and browns of the campagna.

Isabel walks in grove of tall, dark cypresses. A small wind makes a soughing noise in trees as **Isabel** *walks in their cold shade, contemplating the ruins of her happiness. "It had come over her like a high-surging wave that . . . Osmond had married her for her money and Madame Merle had brought about their union."*

81. *Early evening in* **Madame Merle's** *little salon, with its charming artifice and illusion. The two conspirators survey the ruins of their plan.*

MADAME MERLE: I would give my right hand to be able to weep.

OSMOND: What good would it do you to weep?

MADAME MERLE: It would make me feel as I felt before I knew you.

OSMOND: If I've dried up your tears, that's something. But I've seen you shed them.

MADAME MERLE: Oh, I believe you'll make me cry still. I mean make me howl like a wolf. I've a great need of that. I was vile this afternoon. I was horrid.

OSMOND: You may have said things that were in bad taste.

MADAME MERLE: I was full of something bad. I couldn't help it. You've not only dried up my tears, you've dried up my soul. You're *very* bad.

Osmond's studied coldness:

OSMOND: Is this the way we're to end?
MADAME MERLE: How do bad people end? Especially as to their common crimes. You have made me as bad as yourself.

Osmond's conscious indifference gives a strong effect to:

OSMOND: You seem to me quite good enough.

*We have never seen **Madame Merle** so close to losing her self-possession.*

MADAME MERLE: Oh God!

She bends her face, covers it with her hands.

OSMOND: Are you going to weep after all?

Madame Merle doesn't move.

OSMOND: Have I ever complained to you?

Madame Merle drops her hands quickly.

MADAME MERLE: Of course you haven't complained. You've enjoyed your triumph too much. You've made

your wife afraid of you. She was afraid of me this afternoon, but it was really you she feared.

OSMOND: This whole idea didn't originate with me, it
was your genius that brought it about. I only asked that
my wife should like me.

MADAME MERLE: That she should like you so much!

Osmond has picked up a little teacup from the mantel.

OSMOND: If you're determined to make a tragedy of that,
the tragedy's hardly for her. It's for me. I live with the
consequences of it, and so must you.

MADAME MERLE: Please be careful of that precious object.

OSMOND: It already has a wee bit of a tiny crack. However, since my wife doesn't like me I shall look for com-
pensations in Pansy. Fortunately I haven't a fault to find
with her.

82. *The immense ruins of the Colosseum, the great enclosure
half in shadow, on winter afternoon. The fallen, scattered ruins of
stone give a grandly desolate air.*

Rosier watching, across the site:

*Pansy, his little beloved, walking with Isabel towards an open
carriage, framed in one of the massive arches, where the Countess
Gemini sits, waiting for them.*

Rosier starts to run towards them.

Pansy climbing into the carriage, followed by **Isabel**.

ROSIER (*calls*): Mrs. Osmond!

By the time he arrives at the carriage **Isabel** *has given the signal for the carriage to move.*

Pansy and Rosier stare at each other; then **Pansy** *puts her little gloved hands over her eyes, turning her face away.*

Countess Gemini's *avid interest in this handsome little desperado trotting beside their carriage.*

ROSIER: I've been in Paris! I've sold my bibelots! The result's magnificent—fifty thousand dollars! Will Mr. Osmond think me rich enough now?

Isabel's *horror and pity at his useless sacrifice.*

The **Countess** *turns to watch:*

Rosier being left behind, dwarfed by the massive ruins, as the carriage speeds up and pulls away from him.

83. *A nun shepherds* **Pansy** *down staircase of Palazzo Roccanera, moving quickly. They both wear cloaks.*

———

84. *In the dining room a **servant** is removing a fourth place-setting.*

*Isabel joins Osmond and the **Countess Gemini** at the table. The first course and wine are served. Pansy's absence is a vivid presence. Isabel hesitates; then, after a while:*

ISABEL: Is Pansy not well?
OSMOND: No, she is quite well, but I have sent her to the convent. I didn't speak of it to you because I doubt if I can make you understand. One's daughter should be fresh and fair. Pansy's a little dusty, a little dishevelled. She'll have time to think, and there's something I want her to think about.

Osmond deliberate, reasonable. Isabel chilled, she finds it hard to even pretend to eat.

COUNTESS: It's very absurd, my dear Osmond. Why don't you say at once that you want to get her out of my way?

Osmond sips his wine, smiles as if being gallant:

OSMOND: My dear Amy, in that case, it would be much simpler to banish you.
COUNTESS: You know I think very well of Mr. Rosier, I do indeed, he seems to me *simpaticissimo*. He has made me believe in true love.

———

85. *A telegram being handed by telegram **delivery boy**, through an open door of Palazzo Roccanera, to a **manservant**.*

*The telegram, on a silver tray, being carried upstairs by another **manservant**.*

*Isabel taking the telegram from silver tray, with brief thanks in Italian to the manservant. The telegram torn open and quickly scanned by **Isabel**.*

Isabel hurrying down a long, shadowy hallway, daylight thrown intermittently across her as she passes open doors.

86. *Osmond bent to his desk, making a delicate watercolor copy of an antique coin, on immaculate paper, with fine brushes.*

*The door of his study opens behind him and **Isabel** hurries in.*

ISABEL: Excuse me for disturbing you.

Osmond doesn't stop his work, doesn't turn.

OSMOND: When I come into your room I always knock.
ISABEL: I forgot, I had something else to think of. My cousin's dying.

Osmond uses a magnifying glass on his work.

———

OSMOND: I don't believe that. He was dying when we married. He'll outlive us all.

ISABEL: My aunt has telegraphed for me. I must go to England.

OSMOND: I don't see the need of it.

ISABEL: I must see Ralph before he dies.

OSMOND: I shall not like it if you do.

ISABEL: You won't like it if I don't. You like nothing I do or don't do. You pretend to think I lie.

Osmond finally stops work and stands.

OSMOND: That's why you go, then? Not to see your cousin but to take revenge on me.

ISABEL: I know nothing about revenge.

OSMOND: I do. Don't give me an occasion.

ISABEL: You wish immensely that I would commit some folly.

OSMOND: Let it be clear. If you leave Rome today it will be a piece of the most deliberate, the most calculated opposition.

ISABEL: I can't tell you how unjust you seem to me. It's your own opposition that's calculated.

Isabel has never said her worst thoughts to Osmond. Between them they have arrived at a crisis.

ISABEL: It's malignant.

OSMOND: I've an ideal of what my wife should do and should not do. She should not travel across Europe alone, to sit at the bedside of other men. Your cousin's nothing to you, he's nothing to us. You smile most expressively

111

when I talk about us, but I assure you that we, we, Mrs. Osmond, is all I know. You are nearer to me than any human creature, and I'm nearer to you. It may be a disagreeable proximity, but it's one of our own deliberate making. You don't like to be reminded of that, I know, but I'm perfectly willing, because—because I think we should accept the consequences of our actions, and what I value most in life is the honor of a thing.

"Ten minutes before Isabel had felt all the joy of action, but action had been suddenly transformed by the blight of Osmond's touch."

87. *The* **Countess Gemini** *in a small sitting room with a little informal library. She is bored, flicking through books, looking for a diversion.*

88. *Isabel on her way from Osmond's study, back down through series of doorways:* "Her faculties, her energy, her passion, were all dispersed again. She felt as if a cold, dark mist had suddenly encompassed her."

As she passes a doorway, the **Countess Gemini** *appears on the threshold with a book.*

COUNTESS: My dear, do tell me some amusing book to read. Would this do me any good?

*Isabel glances, without seeing, at the book the **Countess** holds out.*

ISABEL: I can't advise you. I've had bad news. My cousin Ralph Touchett is dying.
COUNTESS: Ah, he was so *simpatico*. I'm awfully sorry for you. You look very badly.
ISABEL: Osmond says it's impossible I should go to England.
COUNTESS: Why does Osmond say it's impossible?

Isabel's frank bitterness:

ISABEL: Because we're so happy together that we can't separate even for a fortnight.

*As the **Countess** watches **Isabel** move away, she understands Isabel's trouble is deep and feels an almost "joyous expectation" at the thought of her brother at last being "overtopped."*

89. *Isabel lies sprawled—face hidden, in grief—on a sofa in her private sitting room.*

*Behind her—unheard, unseen by **Isabel**—the **Countess** comes quietly into the room and crosses to the sofa: "a strange smile on her lips, her whole face a shining intimation."*

*She looks down at **Isabel** a moment before:*

COUNTESS: You're very unhappy.

Isabel twists around to look up at the **Countess:**

ISABEL: Yes, but I don't think that you can comfort me.
COUNTESS: Will you give me leave to try?

The **Countess** *joins* **Isabel** *on the sofa. She is smiling, "something exultant in her expression."*

COUNTESS: There's something I want you to know. Perhaps you do, perhaps you've guessed it.

Isabel's sense of foreboding:

ISABEL: What do you wish me to know?

The **Countess** *can't resist delaying a little.*

COUNTESS: In your place I should have guessed it ages ago. Have you never really suspected?
ISABEL: What should I have suspected? I don't know what you mean.
COUNTESS: That's because you've such a beastly pure mind.
ISABEL: You're going to tell me something horrible.

Isabel slowly gets up. The **Countess's** *"gathered perversity grows vivid and dreadful" as she also stands.*

COUNTESS: My first sister-in-law had no children. The poor little woman was married hardly three years and died childless.

Isabel puzzled, trying to follow.

ISABEL: Pansy's not my husband's child then?
COUNTESS: Your husband's in perfection! But not his wife's. My dear Isabel, with you one must dot one's *i*'s.
ISABEL: Whose child?
COUNTESS: She has been wonderfully clever, she has been magnificent, about Pansy.

Isabel gives a long murmur of wonder and understanding. She "feels bruised and scant of breath, her head humming." Weak, she leans for support on the mantel, then drops her "dizzy head, with closed eyes and pale lips, on to her arms."

COUNTESS: At last you understand! Had it never occurred to you that Serena Merle was for six or seven years his lover?
ISABEL: No idea, for me, ever definitely took that form. And Pansy, who doesn't like her.
COUNTESS: She has had a terror lest the mother should betray herself. She has been awfully careful. The mother has never done so.
ISABEL: Yes, yes, the mother has done so. She betrayed herself to me the other day, although I didn't recognize her.

90. *Isabel and her **maid** move around her bedroom, swiftly packing.*

91. *Early winter evening.* **Isabel** *and her* **maid** *in a carriage, through Rome streets.*

92. *In a vast, cold apartment of the convent,* **Isabel** *waits alone.*

The door opens and a **portress** *stands aside to usher someone in.*

To **Isabel**'s *extreme surprise it is not Pansy but* **Madame Merle.** **Isabel** *feels faint.*

MADAME MERLE (*to portress*): You can leave us alone.

After this first brief look, **Isabel** *doesn't look at* **Madame Merle.** *She stands with her back to the room, looking out of the window, unseeing, at the darkening convent garden.*

MADAME MERLE: You're surprised to find me here, and I'm afraid you're not pleased. I confess I've been rather indiscreet, I ought to have asked your permission. I came to see Pansy because it occurred to me this afternoon that she must be rather lonely—

Isabel hears a sudden break in **Madame Merle**'s *voice.*

*"***Madame Merle** *had guessed in the space of an instant that everything was at an end between them, and in the space of another instant she had guessed the reason why.* **Isabel** *knew her secret."*

She falters for only a second.

MADAME MERLE: —that it's a little dismal. So I came—
on the chance—

*Isabel sees "the dry, staring fact that she had been an applied
handled hung-up tool, as senseless and convenient as mere shaped
wood and iron. Her only revenge is to be silent, to leave **Madame
Merle** in this unprecedented position."*

*At last **Madame Merle** sits: "a confession of helplessness."*

93. *A* nun *leads* **Isabel** *up a narrow winding staircase. The
convent is like a "penal establishment."*

94. *The fading evening light shows a crucifix with an ivory
Christ on the wall of Pansy's spartan little cell, with its meager
furniture. It is bitterly cold.*

Pansy *looks around at her few possessions, which she has placed
here and there:*

PANSY: Don't you think I've made it pretty?

Isabel scarcely knows what she can say to the girl.

ISABEL: Yes, it seems comfortable. I've come to bid you
goodbye. I'm going to England.

PANSY: Not to come back?

ISABEL: My cousin is very ill.

PANSY: And will Papa go?

ISABEL: No, I go alone.

PANSY: Don't leave me here.

Isabel silent a moment, rapidly reflecting.

ISABEL: Will you come with me, now?

Pansy looks at her pleadingly.

PANSY: Did Papa tell you to ask me that?

ISABEL: No, it's my own proposal.

PANSY: I had better wait, then. He thinks I have not had enough. But I have. Papa wished me to think a little, and I've thought a great deal.

ISABEL: What have you thought?

PANSY: That I must never displease Papa.

ISABEL: You knew that before.

PANSY: Yes, but I know it better now. I'll do anything —I'll do anything.

Isabel's pity as she sees Pansy has been broken, vanquished.

ISABEL: I must go. I leave Rome tonight.

Pansy holds on to Isabel's dress.

PANSY: You look strange. You frighten me. Perhaps you won't come back?

ISABEL: Perhaps not. I can't tell.

PANSY: Mrs. Osmond, don't leave me!
ISABEL: What can I do for you?
PANSY: I'm a little afraid.
ISABEL: Afraid of what?
PANSY: Of Papa, a little. And of Madame Merle.

95. *Outside the convent, the narrow street is almost dark. Isabel's carriage waiting.*

Isabel comes out of tall door, closing behind her.

As she hurries towards carriage:

Madame Merle steps out of the shadows: "She had recovered her balance, in full possession of her resources."

Isabel startled, even a little frightened.

MADAME MERLE: I found I wished to wait for you. But it's not to talk about Pansy.

Isabel pauses, waiting.

MADAME MERLE: Are you very fond of your cousin?
ISABEL: I don't understand you.

Madame Merle hangs fire.

MADAME MERLE: It's rather hard to explain. Your cousin once did you a great service. Have you never guessed it?

Isabel waits.

MADAME MERLE: He made you rich.
ISABEL: *He* made me?
MADAME MERLE: It was your uncle's money, but it was your cousin's idea. He brought his father over to it.
ISABEL: I don't know why you say such things. I don't know how you know.
MADAME MERLE: I know nothing but what I've guessed. But I've guessed that. At bottom it's him you've to thank.

Isabel stands staring, then goes to her carriage, but stops and turns. Her only revenge:

ISABEL: I believed it was you I had to thank.
MADAME MERLE: You're very unhappy, I know. But I'm more so.
ISABEL: Yes, I can believe that.

As Isabel turns away from her, Madame Merle disappears back into the shadows of the street.

96. *The dusky, smoky, far-arching vault of Charing Cross Station. The strange, livid light and the dense, dark, pushing crowd fill Isabel with a kind of nervous fear. She sees Henrietta and Bantling in the crowd.*

*Isabel, her arm linked in her friend's, shakes hands with **Bantling**.*

BANTLING: How was the Channel?

Isabel barely knows: she made the journey from Rome "with sightless eyes."

ISABEL: Very fine. No, I believe it was very rough.

*Bantling disappears into the crowd to find **Isabel**'s maid and luggage.*

HENRIETTA: Isabel Archer, I have to beg your pardon. You don't know why? Because I criticized you, and yet I've gone further than you. At least Mr. Osmond was born on the other side.

*It takes **Isabel** a moment to grasp her friend's meaning.*

ISABEL: Henrietta Stackpole, are you going to give up your country?
HENRIETTA: Yes, I'm going to marry Mr. Bantling and locate right here in London.
ISABEL: It seems very strange.
HENRIETTA: Well, yes, I suppose it does. I think I know what I'm doing, but I don't know that I can explain.
ISABEL: One can't explain one's marriage.
HENRIETTA: I've come to it little by little. I've studied him for many years and now I see right through him. He's not intellectual, but he appreciates intellect. On the other hand, he doesn't exaggerate its claims. I sometimes think we do in the United States.

ISABEL: You've changed indeed. I hope you'll be very happy.

Henrietta's artless elation: Isabel feels the strange comedy of it.

97. *Gardencourt has the profound stillness of a sick house.*

Isabel wanders down the long drawing room where **Madame Merle** *once played the piano.* **Ralph's** *dogs, fewer now and six years older, trail after her. "She had gone forth in her strength, she came back in her weakness."*

A deep, high window shows the light of a winter day, just before snow, across the grounds.

Distant figure of **Mrs. Touchett,** *in a cloak, wandering across Gardencourt's wintery lawns.*

98. *Mrs. Touchett sees Isabel come out of the house towards her. She gestures her niece back into the house and makes her way up the slope to follow her in.*

———

99. *In the house, Isabel helps Mrs. Touchett off with her cloak.*

ISABEL: Will he sees me? Can he speak to me?
MRS. TOUCHETT: You can try him.
ISABEL: Is there really no hope?
MRS. TOUCHETT: None whatever. There never has been. It has not been a successful life.

Isabel irritated by her aunt's dryness.

ISABEL: No, only a beautiful one.
MRS. TOUCHETT: I don't know what you mean by that, there's no beauty without health.

They walk through the house.

MRS. TOUCHETT: Lord Warburton paid Ralph a visit yesterday. He is engaged to be married.
ISABEL: To be married! Are you sure?
MRS. TOUCHETT: I can't be surer than he, but he seemed sure.
ISABEL: Who is he marrying?
MRS. TOUCHETT: Lady Flora, Lady Felicia, something of that sort.

Isabel aware of Mrs. Touchett's "gaze like a gimlet."

100. *Towards evening in* **Ralph's** *sickroom. Two* **nurses** *with him. His favorite hound in attendance. A fire burning.*

Ralph, drifting in and out of consciousness, opens his eyes:

RALPH: . . . Isabel . . . has come . . .

101. *One of the **nurses**, keeping the dogs below, watches as **Isabel** hurries up the stairs.*

102. *Twilight slowly fading in **Ralph's** room.*

*Isabel alone with **Ralph**.*

His face as still as the lid of a box, eyes closed: "the figure and pattern of death."

Isabel sees his hand move, searching for her presence. She takes his hand in hers.

*He opens his eyes, looking at her. **Isabel** feels "as if she is looking into immeasurable space."*

Ralph's voice, slow, with painful breaks and pauses, seems to come from a distance.

RALPH: It was very good of you to come. I thought you would, but I wasn't sure.

ISABEL: I was not sure either, until I came.
RALPH: With me it's all over.

Isabel bows her head further, until it rests on her hands clasped over his.

RALPH: Isabel, I wish it were over for you.

He listens to her crying, then groans.

RALPH: What is it you have done for me, in leaving Rome?

Isabel's agitation: she looks up, she has lost all shame, all wish to hide things.

ISABEL: What is it you did for me? You did something once—you know it. Oh, Ralph, you've been everything. What have I done for you? I would die if you could live.

Her voice as broken as his own.

RALPH: Keep me in your heart. I shall be nearer to you than I've ever been.
ISABEL: I've never thanked you—I never spoke—I never was what I should be. Yet how could I know? I only know today because there are people less stupid than I.
RALPH: Don't mind people.
ISABEL: Is it true—is it true?
RALPH (*humorous*): That you've been stupid? Oh no.
ISABEL: That you made me rich—that all I have is yours?

Ralph turns away his head, for a long time says nothing.

RALPH: Don't speak of that—that was not happy.

He turns his head to look at her again.

RALPH: But for that—but for that!—I believe I ruined you.

For **Isabel** *nothing matters now but the knowledge that they are looking at the truth together.*

ISABEL: He married me for the money. I only want you to understand. I always tried to keep you from understanding, but that's all over.

Isabel presses her lips to the back of his hand.

RALPH: I always understood, though it was so strange—so pitiful. You wanted to look at life for yourself, but you were not allowed. You were punished for your wish.
ISABEL: Oh yes, I've been punished.

Ralph listens to **Isabel** *crying.*

RALPH: Was he very bad about your coming?
ISABEL: He made it very hard for me. But I don't care.
RALPH: Is it all over between you?
ISABEL: I don't know—I can't tell. Here—with you—I'm happier than I have been for a long time. I want you to be happy—to feel that I'm near you and that I

love you. Why should there be pain? That's not the deepest thing.

RALPH: You must stay here. Pain's deep, but it passes, after all. It's passing now. But love remains. I don't know why we should suffer so much. Perhaps I shall find out. There are many things in life. You're very young.

ISABEL: I feel very old.

RALPH: I don't believe—

His strength fails him, then:

RALPH: I don't believe that such a generous mistake as yours can hurt you for more than a little.

Isabel's tears, her happiness.

RALPH: And remember this, that if you've been hated you've also been loved. Ah, but Isabel—*adored!*

Isabel prostrated deep, deeper on the bed, closer to him than she has ever been.

103.   *Isabel in the same room she first had at Gardencourt.*

Cold, faint dawn. Profound silence of house.

———

127

Isabel fully dressed on the bed, eyes open. Then, as abruptly as if someone had called her, she sits up.

*For a second she senses **Ralph** at the foot of her bed. But she sees there is no one there.*

104. *Isabel hurries along a cold, dark corridor.*

Down a flight of narrow, winding oak stairs, gleaming in dawn's early light.

105. *Mrs. Touchett beside **Ralph**'s bed, his hand in hers.*

*Behind her, **Isabel** comes into the room.*

*The **doctor**, facing **Isabel**, holds **Ralph**'s wrist, then puts his hand back. Two **nurses** at the foot of the bed. Not a word said.*

Isabel goes to Mrs. Touchett and puts an arm around her.

*For a second **Mrs. Touchett** allows this embrace: "She was stiff and dry-eyed, her acute white face was terrible."*

ISABEL: Dear Aunt Lydia.
MRS. TOUCHETT: Go and thank God you've no child.

*And she disengages herself from **Isabel**'s touch.*

106. *Three days later, in the coldness that comes before snow, a small **congregation** files out of a gray stone church, behind **Ralph**'s coffin. **Warburton** is one of the bearers, **Bantling** another.*

*As the group goes towards the little graveyard next to the church, we see among them: **Isabel**, **Mrs. Touchett**, a crying **Henrietta**, and **Caspar Goodwood**.*

*The **minister** stands at the head of the grave. We hear the **minister** speak the words of the burial service. The coffin being prepared to be lowered in to the freshly dug, almost frozen soil. **Isabel** won't meet **Caspar**'s look, more intense than is usual in public. He makes her uneasy.*

107. *The last of the light across Gardencourt's ground.*

***Isabel**, still wearing her clothes from the funeral, wanders under the great winter trees.*

***Isabel** wanders into the little rustic arbor where **Lord Warburton** proposed. She stands, looking around her. Then, with an absolute absence of purpose, she sits on the rustic stone bench.*

A few almost imperceptible flakes of snow start to fall.

As the twilight deepens and shadows gather around her, she has a sense that she is not alone. She glances around quickly and sees:

Caspar Goodwood, a little way off, staring at her.

She stands as Caspar crosses to her.

He holds her wrist and forces her, with just a touch, back down onto the bench. There is "something in his face she wishes not to see."

ISABEL: You frightened me.

Her feeling of danger as Caspar speaks:

CASPAR: I wanted to see you alone. So I've been waiting and walking about. I want to speak to you. I don't want to trouble you, as I did in Rome. That was of no use, it only distressed you. I knew I was wrong, but I'm not wrong now. It's very different, now I can help you.

Isabel "listens to him as she had never listened before: his words dropped deep into her soul." She finds it almost an effort to speak.

ISABEL: How can you help me?
CASPAR: It was a good thing when you made me come away with your cousin. He was a good man, a fine man. He told me how the case stands for you. He explained everything, he guessed my sentiments. Do you know what he said to me, here, the last time I saw him? He said, "Do everything you can for her, do everything she'll let you."

Isabel abruptly stands.

ISABEL: You had no business to talk about me.

Caspar follows her, quickly standing.

CASPAR: Why not? Why not, when we talked in that way?
And he was dying.

Isabel falters, stops, listens.

CASPAR: How can you pretend you're not heartbroken?
It's too late to play a part—didn't you leave all that
behind you in Rome? Touchett knew, and I knew what
it cost you to come here. It will have cost you your life.

He is now almost angry.

CASPAR: Give me one word of truth! You're afraid to go
back. You're perfectly alone. You don't know where to
turn. Now I want you to think of *me*.
ISABEL: To think of you?
CASPAR: Turn to me. Why should you go back—why
should you go through that ghastly form?
ISABEL (*frightened*): To get away from you.
CASPAR: I want to prevent that, if you'll only for once
listen to me. Why shouldn't we be happy—when it's here
before us, when it's so easy? You took the great step in
coming away—the next is nothing, it's the natural one. I
know how you suffer, and that's why I'm here. We can
do absolutely as we please. To whom under the sun do
we owe anything?

Isabel gives a long murmur, a creature of pain.

ISABEL: I beg you to go away!
CASPAR: Don't say that, don't kill me.

Caspar holds her, embraces her, body to body, kisses her. Isabel responds: a full sexual awareness.

They part.

Isabel hurries away from Caspar.

Snow now falling more rapidly, covering the ground.

Lights far away in the windows of the house.

Isabel hurries across the dark grounds—through darkening light and denser darkness under trees—towards the house lights, casting their light far out across the snowy lawns.

Isabel's anger: she now fully realizes the arid darkness of the prison-castle Osmond has created around her. In her determination to salvage something from it "there was a very straight path."

At the door she pauses.

She looks all around her: into the dark snowy grounds, the lit house behind her. She listens.

She puts her hand on the door latch.

———

108. *The hallway of a London house in midday light.*

Henrietta, in coat, putting on her hat. Sound of door knocker.

*Henrietta, ignoring the **maid** who appears behind her, goes to the door and opens it to:*

Caspar Goodwood.

CASPAR: Good morning. I hoped to find Mrs. Osmond here.

Henrietta pauses, before:

HENRIETTA: She came here last night. But she left again this morning.
CASPAR: She left—?

*He can't look at **Henrietta**—he stiffly averts his face—but nor can he otherwise move.*

109. *A carriage moves through narrow, winding Roman streets. Isabel's face pale in darkness. Sound of horses.*

110. *Pansy in her little lamplit cell.*

She sits in the shadows: silent, patient.

The door opens.

PORTRESS: A visitor to see you.

Isabel comes into the room.

The door shuts behind her.

Isabel steps into the lamplight.

Pansy looks at her as if at an apparition. Pansy's voice out of the shadows:

PANSY: You've come back.

Isabel—eyes dazzled by light—finds it hard to see the girl in the shadows beyond the lamplight.

ISABEL: Yes, I've come for you.

She holds out her hands towards Pansy.

Pansy sees Isabel's hands, held out, in the brightest part of the light.

The End

The Portrait of a Lady

THE CAST

Isabel Archer	Nicole Kidman
Gilbert Osmond	John Malkovich
Madame Merle	Barbara Hershey
Henrietta Stackpole	Mary-Louise Parker
Ralph Touchett	Martin Donovan
Mrs. Touchett	Shelley Winters
Lord Warburton	Richard E. Grant
Countess Gemini	Shelley Duvall
Edward Rosier	Christian Bale
Caspar Goodwood	Viggo Mortensen
Mr. Touchett	Sir John Gielgud
Pansy Osmond	Valentina Cervi

Character Notes

The following notes were extracted from the novel (Henry James, **The Portrait of a Lady**. New York: Penguin Books, 1986) specifically for the actors, to help them to get into their characters, or to use as a reminder once they had read the novel. The various paragraphs for each character come from different parts of the novel.

Isabel Archer

It may be affirmed that Isabel was probably very liable to the sin of self-esteem; she often surveyed with complacency the field of her own nature; she was in the habit of taking for granted, on scanty evidence, that she was right; she treated herself to occasions of homage. Meanwhile her errors and delusions were frequently such as a biographer interested in preserving the dignity of his subject must shrink from specifying. Her thoughts were a tangle of vague outlines which had never been corrected by the judgment of people speaking with authority. In matters of opinion she had had her own way, and it had led her into a thousand ridiculous zig-zags. At moments she discovered she was grotesquely wrong, and then she treated herself to a week of passionate humility. After this she held her head higher than ever again; for it was of no use, she had an unquenchable desire to think well of herself.

Deep in her soul—it was the deepest thing there—lay a belief that if a certain light should dawn she could give herself completely; but this image, on the whole, was too formidable to be attractive. Isabel's thoughts hovered about it, but they seldom rested on it for long; after a little it ended in alarms. It often seemed to her that she thought too much about herself; you could have made her colour, any day in the year, by calling her a rank egoist. She was always planning out her development, desiring her perfection, observing her progress. Her nature had, in her conceit, a certain garden-like quality, a suggestion of perfume and murmuring boughs, of shady bowers and lengthening vistas, which made her feel that introspection was, after all, an exercise in the open air, and that a visit to the recesses of one's spirit was harmless when she returned from it with a lapful of roses. But she was often reminded that there were other gardens in the world than those of her remarkable soul, and that there were moreover a great many places which were not gardens at all—only dusky pestiferous tracts, planted thick with ugliness and misery.

Ralph Touchett

Tall, lean, loosely and feebly put together, he had an ugly, sickly, witty, charming face, furnished, but by no means decorated, with a straggling moustache and whisker. He looked clever and ill—a combination by no means felicitous; and he wore a brown velvet jacket. He carried his hands in his pockets, and there was something in the way he did it that showed the habit was inveterate. His gait has a shambling, wandering quality, he was not very firm on his legs.

He was assured he might outweather a dozen winters if he would betake himself to those climates in which consumptives chiefly congregate. As he had grown extremely fond of London, he cursed the flatness of exile; but at the same time that he cursed he conformed, and gradually, when he found his sensitive organ grateful even for grim favours, he conferred them with a lighter hand. He wintered abroad, as the phrase is; basked in the sun, stopped at home when the wind blew, went to bed when it rained, and once or twice, when it snowed overnight, almost never got up again.

Living as he now lived was like reading a good book in a poor translation—a meagre entertainment for a young man who felt that he might have been an excellent linguist.

Gilbert Osmond

Mr Osmond had a well-bred air of expecting nothing, a quiet ease that covered everything, even the first show of his own wit. This was the more grateful as his face, his head, was sensitive; he was not handsome, but he was fine, as fine as one of the drawings in the long gallery above the bridge of the Uffizi. And his very voice was fine—the more strangely that, with its clearness, it yet somehow wasn't sweet.

He was an original without being an eccentric. His sensibility had governed him—possibly governed him too much; it made him impatient of vulgar troubles and had led him to live by himself, in a sorted, sifted, arranged world, thinking about art and beauty and history. He had consulted his taste in everything—his taste alone perhaps, as a sick man consciously incurable consults at last only his lawyer: that was what made him so different from everyone else.

Contentment, on his part, took no vulgar form; excitement, in the most self-conscious of men, was a kind of ecstasy of self-control. This disposition, however, made him an admirable lover; it gave him a constant view of the smitten and dedicated state. He never forgot himself, as I say; and so he never forgot to be graceful and tender, to wear the appearance—which presented indeed no difficulty—of stirred senses and deep intentions.

Madame Merle

She was forty years old and not pretty, though her expression charmed.

She had known great things and great people, but she had never played a great part. She was one of the small ones of the earth; she had not been born to honours; she knew the world too well to nourish fatuous illusions on the article of her own place in it. She had encountered many of the fortunate few and was perfectly aware of those points at which their fortune differed from hers.

She was never weary, never overcome with disgust; she never appeared to need rest or consolation. She had her own ideas; she had of old exposed a great many of them to Isabel, who knew also that under an appearance of extreme self-control her highly-cultivated friend concealed a rich sensibility. But her will was mistress of her life; there was something gallant in the way she kept going. It was as if she had learned the secret of it—as if the art of life were some clever trick she had guessed.

Mrs. Touchett

She was a plain-faced old woman, without graces and without any great elegance, but with an extreme respect for her own motives. The edges of her conduct were so clear-cut that for susceptible persons it sometimes had a knife-like effect. She was virtually separated from her husband, but she appeared to perceive nothing irregular in the situation.

Mrs Touchett indulged in no regrets nor speculations, and usually came once a year to spend a month with her husband, a period during which she apparently took pains to convince him that she had adopted the right system. She was not fond of the English style of life, and has three or four reasons for it to which she currently alluded; they bore upon minor points of that ancient order, but for Mrs Touchett they amply justified non-residence. She detested bread-sauce, which, as she said, looked like a poultice and tasted like soap; she objected to the consumption of beer by her maid-servants; and affirmed that the British laundress (Mrs Touchett was very particular about the appearance of her linen) was not a mistress of her art.

Mrs Touchett had a great merit; she was as honest as a pair of compasses. There was a comfort in her stiffness and firmness; you knew exactly where to find her and were never liable to chance encounters and concussions. On her own ground she was perfectly present, but was never over-inquisitive as regards the territory of her neighbour.

Daniel Touchett saw before him a life-long residence in his adopted country, of which from the first, he took a simple, sane and accommodating view. But, as he said to himself, he had no intention of disamericanizing, nor had he a desire to teach his only son any subtle art.

Now he was taking the rest that precedes the great rest. He had a narrow, clean-shaven face, with features evenly distributed and an expression of placid acuteness. It was evidently a face in which the range of representation was not large, so that the air of contented shrewdness was all the more of a merit.

Lord Warburton

He was a remarkably well-made man of five-and-thirty; a noticeably handsome face, fresh-coloured, fair and frank, with firm, straight features, a lively grey eye and the rich adornment of a chestnut beard. This person had a certain fortunate, brilliant exceptional look—the air of a happy temperament fertilized by a high civilization—which would have made almost any observer envy him at a venture.

"Lord Warburton's a very amicable young man—a very fine young man. He has a hundred thousand a year. He owns fifty thousand acres of the soil of this little island and ever so many other things besides. He has half a dozen houses to live in. He has a seat in Parliament as I have one at my own dinner-table. He has elegant tastes—cares for literature, for art, for science, for charming young ladies. The most elegant is his taste for the new views." (Daniel Touchett)

She was a neat, plump person, of medium stature, with a round face, a small mouth, a delicate complexion, a bunch of light brown ringlets at the back of her head and a peculiarly open, surprised-looking eye. The most striking point in her appearance was the remarkable fixedness of this organ, which rested without impudence or defiance, but as if in conscientious exercise of a natural right, upon every object it happened to encounter.

Henrietta was in the van of progress and had clear-cut views on most subjects; her cherished desire had long been to come to Europe and write a series of letters to the *Interviewer* from the radical point of view—an enterprise the less difficult as she knew perfectly in advance what her opinions would be and how many objections most European institutions lay open.

"Miss Stackpole, however, is our most wonderful invention. She strikes me as a kind of monster. One hasn't a nerve in one's body that she doesn't set quivering. You know I never have admitted that she's a woman. Do you know what she reminds me of? Of a new steel pen—the most odious thing in nature. She talks as a steel pen writes; aren't her letters, by the way, on ruled paper?" (Gilbert Osmond)

Mr. Bantling

Mr. Bantling, a stout, sleek, smiling man of forty, wonderfully dressed, universally informed and incoherentely amused, laughed immoderately at everything Henrietta said.

He assured her that he was often very blue, and that when he was blue he was awfully fierce.

Caspar Goodwood

The name of the gentleman was Caspar Goodwood; he was a straight young man from Boston; he was tall, strong and somewhat stiff; he was also lean and brown. He was not romantically, he was much rather obscurely, handsome, but his physiognomy had an air of requesting your attention, which it rewarded according to the charm you found in blue eyes of remarkable fixedness; the eyes of a complexion other than his own, and a jaw of the somewhat angular mould which is supposed to bespeak resolution.

He was not, it may be added, a man weakly to accept defeat.

Countess Gemini

The Countess Gemini arrived with her trunks, her dresses, her chatter, her falsehoods, her frivolity, the strange, the unholy legend of the number of her lovers.

She was often extremely bored—bored, in her own phrase, to extinction. She had not been extinguished, however, and she struggled bravely enough with her destiny, which had been to marry an unaccommodating Florentine.

She had always observed that she got on better with clever women than silly ones like herself; the silly ones could never understand her wisdom; whereas the clever ones—the really clever ones—always understood her silliness.

Pansy Osmond

Pansy was really a blank page, a pure white surface, successfully kept so; she had neither art, nor guile, nor temper, nor talent—only two or three small exquisite instincts: for knowing a friend, for avoiding a mistake, for taking care of an old toy or new frock. Yet to be so tender was to be touching withal, and she could be felt as an easy victim of fate. She would have no will, no power to resist, no sense of her own importance; she would easily be mystified, easily crushed: her force would be all in knowing when and where to cling.

Edward Rosier

There was still something agreeable to the nostrils about him and something not offensive to nobler organs. He was a very gentle and gracious youth, with what are called cultivated tastes—an acquaintance with old china, with good wine, with the bindings of books, with the *Almanach de Gotha*, with the best shops, the best hotels, the hours of railway-trains.

Actor Biographies

Nicole Kidman

Nicole Kidman plays the title role in *The Portrait of a Lady*, that of Isabel Archer.

Nicole Kidman first came to the attention of American audiences with her critically acclaimed performance in the riveting 1989 psychological thriller *Dead Calm*. Since then, she has become one of the most sought-after young actresses in film.

Recently she has starred as Suzanne Stone in director Gus Van Sant's widely acclaimed black comedy *To Die For*. For her pitch-perfect, wickedly funny portrayal of a woman obsessed with the dream of becoming a TV personality, she won a Best Actress Golden Globe Award in 1996, along with Best Actress awards from the Boston Film Critics, the Seattle Film Festival, the Broadcast Film Critics, and London's *Empire* magazine. She was also nominated by BAFTA, the London Film Critics, and the American Comedy Awards. This followed her role as Dr. Chase Meridian opposite Val Kilmer in Joel Schumacher's hit feature *Batman Forever*, for which she won the Blockbuster Award for Best Female in an Action/Adventure.

Since completing *The Portrait of a Lady*, she has starred opposite George Clooney in the first DreamWorks production, *The Peacemaker*. In the fall of 1996 she and Tom Cruise went before the cameras in England for director Stanley Kubrick in the movie *Eyes Wide Shut*.

In the latter part of 1993, Kidman appeared opposite Alec

Baldwin in Harold Becker's thriller *Malice*, followed by the starring role opposite Michael Keaton in the drama *My Life*. Other film credits include roles opposite Tom Cruise in Ron Howard's *Far and Away* and Tony Scott's *Days of Thunder*, and opposite Dustin Hoffman in Robert Benton's screen version of *Billy Bathgate*, for which she received a Golden Globe nomination.

Born in Hawaii, Kidman spent her childhood in Australia with parents who instilled in her a love of culture and education. Her father is a lecturer in biochemistry and her mother is a nurse/educator. Kidman studied ballet as a young child and enrolled in drama school at age ten. She made her debut in an Australian film, *Bush Christmas*, at fourteen, and afterward began finding almost continuous work.

She appeared in projects such as *Winners* and the Disney Channel miniseries *Five-Mile Creek*, in which she appeared as a "little roughie who herded sheep."

Between films, Kidman honed her craft at the Australian Theatre for Young People in Sydney and the Philip Street Theatre, where she learned voice and production and studied theater history.

The much-lauded 1985 Kennedy-Miller miniseries *Vietnam* made her a virtual overnight star in Australia. Only seventeen at the time, she was voted Best Actress of the Year by the Australian public and the Australian Film Institute for her performance. In addition to public and critical acclaim, her performance in the series also attracted the attention of filmmakers throughout Australia.

Her subsequent portrayal of the terrorized wife in *Dead Calm*, a film directed by Philip Noyce and co-starring Sam Neill, was praised by critics both in Australia and abroad.

Following the success of *Dead Calm*, Kidman reunited with the Kennedy-Miller production team for a second acclaimed miniseries, *Bangkok Hilton*. Once again Kidman received rave reviews for her performance (opposite Denholm Elliott) and was voted Best Actress of 1989 by the Variety Awards and once again the Australian public.

Her other notable Australian films include *Emerald City* (for which she received a Best Supporting Actress nomination from the Australian Film Institute) and *Flirting* (the sequel to *The Year My Voice Broke*). She also appeared on stage playing lead roles in *Steel Magnolias* at the Sydney Seymour Centre, for which she was nominated Best Newcomer by the Sydney Theatre Critics, and *Spring Awakening* at the Australian Theatre for Young People.

John Malkovich

John Malkovich, one of America's most gifted actors of stage and screen, plays the role of Gilbert Osmond, the expatriate dilettante whom Isabel Archer marries.

Malkovich was born in Benton, Illinois. Directly out of college, he joined the famed Steppenwolf Theatre Company of Chicago. Between 1976 and 1982, he acted in, directed, or designed the sets for more than fifty Steppenwolf productions. His debut on the New York stage in the Steppenwolf production of Sam Shepard's *True West* earned him an Obie award. Other notable stage credits include *Death of a Salesman*, *Slip of the Tongue*, Sam Shepard's *State of Shock*, Lanford Wilson's *Burn This*, and his own adaptation of Don DeLillo's novel *Libra*.

Malkovich has made his mark on film audiences in features such as Roland Joffe's *The Killing Fields*, Robert Benton's *Places in the Heart*, Steven Spielberg's *Empire of the Sun*, Stephen Frears's *Dangerous Liaisons*, Bernardo Bertolucci's *The Sheltering Sky*, and Wolfgang Petersen's *In the Line of Fire*.

More recently he has worked with top European directors Manoel de Oliveira (*The Convent*, 1995) and Michelangelo Antonioni (*Beyond the Clouds*, 1995). His latest movies include Stephen Frears's *Mary Reilly*, Lee Tamahori's *Mulholland Falls*, and Volker Schlondorff's *The Ogre*.

Sir John Gielgud

One of Britain's best-loved actors, Sir John Gielgud plays Ralph's father, Mr. Touchett, whose generosity allows Isabel to embark upon her adventure.

Gielgud has combined a glittering stage career, both as actor and as director, with increasingly successful film and television ventures. He won the Best Supporting Actor Academy Award for his role as Dudley Moore's butler in *Arthur*, and is well remembered for his contributions to films as diverse as *The Elephant Man*, *Chariots of Fire*, *Gandhi*, *The Shooting Party*, *Plenty*, and *Shining Through*. The television miniseries has also benefited from his august presence: *War and Remembrance*, *Brideshead Revisited*, *Inside the Third Reich*, *Wagner*, *QB VII*, *The Far Pavilions*, *Scarlett*, and *Summer's Lease* among them.

Born in 1904, Gielgud made his stage debut at age nineteen with one line in *Henry V*. He rapidly developed a reputation as an extraordinary performer of the Shakespearean canon, creating a sensation with his youthful Hamlet in 1930. During the 1920s and 1930s, he played Romeo, King Lear, Macbeth, Prospero, Anthony, Oberon, and his favorite, Richard II. As director of *Romeo and Juliet*, he also alternated the roles of Romeo and Mercutio with Laurence Olivier.

Gielgud excels at comedy—in his youth he appeared in Noël Coward's *The Vortex* and *The Constant Nymph*, and he played John Worthing in *The Importance of Being Earnest*.

During World War II, Gielgud entertained the troops with tours of *Hamlet* and *Blithe Spirit* and, in the 1950s, he enjoyed great success in the commercial theater in hits like *The Lady's Not for Burning* and *Five Finger Exercise*. He devoted much of the 1960s to a world tour of his solo recital, *Ages of Man*, and in the 1970s, he collaborated with Ralph Richardson in productions of David Storey's *Home* and Harold Pinter's *No Man's Land*.

Gielgud made his film debut in 1924 with *Who Is That Man*, followed by noteworthy roles in *The Secret Agent*, *Julius Caesar* (as Cassius to Marlon Brando's Mark Anthony), *Richard III*, *The Barretts of Wimpole Street*, *Saint Joan*, *Becket* (earning an Academy Award nomination as King Louis VII opposite Richard Burton and Peter O'Toole), *Chimes at Midnight*, *The Shoes of the Fisherman*, *Julius Caesar* (the title role this time in 1970), *Galileo*, *Murder on the Orient Express*, *Providence*, *11 Harrowhouse*, *The Human Factor*, *The Formula*, Andrzej Wajda's *The Conductor*, *Shining Through*, Peter Greenaway's controversial *Prospero's Books*, and *The Power of One*. He has recently appeared in *First Knight* and *Haunted*.

Gielgud was knighted in 1953 for service to the arts. He published three volumes of autobiography, *Early Stages* in 1953, *Distinguished Company* in 1972, and *An Actor and His Times* in 1979.

Barbara Hershey

Barbara Hershey stars as the enigmatic Madame Merle.

As an actress who has consistently challenged herself, she has to her credit a remarkable array of roles that have garnered her rave reviews and the unprecedented honor of winning the Best Actress Award at the Cannes Film Festival two years in a row, in 1987 for *Shy People* and in 1988 for *A*

World Apart. Most recently, Barbara has featured in *The Pall-bearer* and *Last of the Dogmen*.

A Hollywood native, Barbara was discovered by a talent agent in a student production at Hollywood High School. She debuted in the television series *The Monroes* and made her film debut in the 1968 movie *With Six You Get Eggroll*. Barbara's career moved to a new level with a challenging run of roles in Martin Scorsese's *Boxcar Bertha*, Richard Rush's *The Stunt Man*, Philip Kaufman's *The Right Stuff*, and Barry Levinson's *The Natural*.

It was, however, her role as Lee in Woody Allen's *Hannah and Her Sisters* that brought Barbara to the forefront of to-day's most sought-after and respected actresses. She fol-lowed it with *Hoosiers*, *Tin Men*, *Shy People*, and *A World Apart*. She worked again with Martin Scorsese playing Mary Mag-delene in his extraordinary, controversial adaptation of *The Last Temptation of Christ*. She then appeared in *Beaches*, op-posite Bette Midler, *Tune in Tomorrow* (aka *Aunt Julia and the Scriptwriter*), *Defenseless*, and as a glamorous 1940s nightclub owner in *The Public Eye*.

In 1993, Barbara had four films released. She portrayed the mother of a young man caught up in the world of jazz in pre–World War II Germany in *Swing Kids*, a nympho-maniac duchess in *Splitting Heirs*, the wife of a psychopath in *Falling Down*, and opposite Debra Winger in *A Dangerous Woman*.

Barbara's work for television is no less stellar then her feature film credits. Following her Emmy- and Golden Globe Award–winning performance as a suburban ax mur-deress in *A Killing in a Small Town*, she tackled the role of Dennis Hopper's abused wife in *Paris Trout* (which was re-leased theatrically outside the U.S.), and received another Emmy nomination. She also portrayed a Marilyn Monroe–wannabe sociopath in the miniseries *Stay the Night*. Her most recent television performances include *The Return of Lonesome Dove* for ABC and *Abraham* for TNT.

Mary-Louise Parker

Mary-Louise Parker, one of today's brightest and hottest young actresses, plays Henrietta.

She first achieved critical success in 1992 when she appeared in two of the year's major releases. She co-starred with Mary Stuart Masterson, Jessica Tandy, and Kathy Bates in Jon Avnet's *Fried Green Tomatoes*. She also appeared alongside Steve Martin, Kevin Kline, Mary McDonnell, Alfre Woodard, and Danny Glover in the comedy-drama *Grand Canyon*, directed by Lawrence Kasdan.

Mary-Louise Parker was recently seen in Norman Rene's *Reckless* and with Whoopi Goldberg and Drew Barrymore in *Boys on the Side* for director Herbert Ross. Her past film releases include *Naked in New York*, Anthony Minghella's *Mr. Wonderful*, *The Client*, with Susan Sarandon and Tommy Lee Jones, and Woody Allen's *Bullets over Broadway*.

Parker's other credits include *Signs of Life*, directed by John David Coles, and Norman Rene's highly acclaimed *Longtime Companion*.

In April 1994, Parker was seen in the Hallmark Hall of Fame telefilm *A Place for Annie*, which aired on ABC. She played a drug addict and AIDS victim who gave up her AIDS baby for adoption, only to have second thoughts when she conquers her drug habit.

As Rita in the Craig Lucas–Norman Rene Broadway production of *Prelude to a Kiss*, Parker received a Tony nomination. Most recently, on stage, she played Brenda in the critically acclaimed Manhattan Theater Club production of *Four Dogs and a Bone*. Her other stage credits include *Throwing*

Your Voice at the Ensemble Studio Theater, *Babylon Gardens* opposite Timothy Hutton at the Circle Repertory Company, *Prelude to a Kiss* at the Berkeley Repertory, *The Importance of Being Earnest* at the Hartford Stage, *Up in Saratoga* at the Old Globe, *The Miser* at the Syracuse Stage, *Hayfever* at Studi Arena, *The Night of the Iguana* at the Hartman, *The Age of Pie* and *The Girl in Pink* at the Edge Theater.

Parker last appeared on Broadway in William Inge's *Bus Stop* for the Circle in the Square Theater opposite Billy Crudup. She also recently starred for HBO in John Smith's *Sugartime*.

Martin Donovan

Martin Donovan, who has worked frequently with American independent director Hal Hartley, here plays Ralph Touchett, Isabel's cousin and admirer.

Donovan has recently been seen on film in Hal Hartley's *Amateur* as Thomas, a once brutal criminal who suffers from amnesia. He received the Fort Lauderdale Film Festival's Best Actor award for his performance in the role.

Amateur was Donovan's fourth film with Hartley. Previously, he co-starred with Adrienne Shelly in the award-winning *Trust*, played the lead in the short *Surviving Desire*, and appeared in a brief supporting part in *Simple Men*. He subsequently played a role in the first segment of Hartley's three-part feature, *Flirt*. Originally from Reseda, California, Donovan studied acting at the American Theater of Arts in Los Angeles, where he appeared in such plays as *Richard Cork's Leg* by Brendan Behan and Brecht's *Private Life of the Master Race*. He moved to New York in 1983 and appeared as Josh in Rick King's film *Hard Choices*. He has also appeared in the miniseries *At Mother's Request, Legwork*, and *At*

King's Crossing. His other films include Spike Lee's *Malcolm X*, John Flynn's *Scam* with Christopher Walken, and Michael Almereyda's droll vampire saga, *Nadja*. He is a member of Cucaracha Theater in New York, where he has appeared in more than a half dozen new works, most notably Richard Caliban's *Famine Plays* and *Homo Sapien Shuffle*.

Just before *The Portrait of a Lady*, he completed filming *The Hollow Reed*, directed by Angela Pope and co-starring Ian Hart and Joely Richardson.

Shelley Winters

Shelley Winters is recognized around the world as one of America's most respected actresses. In *The Portrait of a Lady*, she plays Mrs. Touchett, Ralph's mother and Isabel's aunt.

Scores of awards, among them two Academy Awards, four Academy Award nominations, a British Academy Award, Italy's Donatello Award, a Golden Globe, and an Emmy attest to her great talent and versatility in a long career in motion pictures, theater, and television.

She has been seen on the big screen most recently in Paul Mazursky's *The Pickle*, co-starring Danny Aiello, and James Mangold's *Heavy*, co-starring Liv Tyler and Pruitt Taylor Vince.

Shelley first gained attention as Ronald Colman's victimized waitress in *A Double Life* under the direction of George Cukor. She convinced director George Stevens that she could portray the plain factory worker who vies with the upper-class Elizabeth Taylor for Montgomery Clift in *A Place in the Sun*, hailed by critics as one of the greatest films of all time. Shelley's portrayal garnered her first Oscar nomination for Best Actress.

Shelley's prominence was now firmly established, leading

to many other important films, including Charles Laughton's classic *Night of the Hunter* with Robert Mitchum, and *I Am a Camera* with Laurence Harvey. Shelley received her first Oscar for her luminous performance in *The Diary of Anne Frank*, directed by George Stevens. Her second Oscar was for her vicious portrayal of the mother of a blind girl in *A Patch of Blue* with Sidney Poitier.

During this period, Shelley also starred in such films as *Let No Man Write My Epitaph*. She made an indelible impression as the pathetically lovelorn Charlotte Haze in Stanley Kubrick's *Lolita* and appeared in *The Balcony*, *Time of Indifference*, and George Stevens's *The Greatest Story Ever Told*.

She won the British Academy Award for her performance in the landmark British film *Alfie* opposite Michael Caine. She followed this with *Enter Laughing*; *Wild in the Streets*; *Buona Sera, Mrs. Campbell*; and *Bloody Mama*. *The Poseidon Adventure* with its all-star cast brought the disaster genre back with a big box-office bang. The film, directed by Ronald Neame, brought Shelley numerous accolades and her fourth Oscar nomination. Her other films include *Blume in Love, Diamonds, Journey into Fear, The Lucky Touch, The Tenant, Un Borghese Piccolo Piccolo, Pete's Dragon, The Delta Force, An Unremarkable Life, Touch of a Stranger,* and *Stepping Out.*

Shelley has returned to the stage many times during her busy film career and is also the author of *One Night Stand of a Noisy Passenger*, which was produced off Broadway. In addition, she has written two best-selling autobiographies, *Shelley* and *Shelley II.* She has spent many years teaching acting to youngsters at the Actors Studio in New York and Los Angeles.

Richard E. Grant

Richard E. Grant, one of Britain's most popular actors, plays Lord Warburton, another of Isabel Archer's many admirers.

Grant first attracted moviegoers' attention in 1986 in Bruce Robinson's cult movie *Withnail and I.* As the flamboyant Withnail, an unemployed actor at the end of the 1960s, Grant was able to display both his comic and dramatic talents to the full.

In the last ten years, he has appeared in a number of major British and American movies, such as Philip Kaufman's *Henry and June,* Bob Rafelson's *Mountains of the Moon,* Bruce Robinson's *How to Get Ahead in Advertising,* Michael Lehman's *Hudson Hawk,* Francis Ford Coppola's *Dracula,* Robert Altman's *The Player,* Martin Scorsese's *The Age of Innocence,* Tim Sullivan's *Jack and Sarah,* and Robert Altman's *Pret a Porter* (aka *Ready to Wear*). He will shortly be seen in Trevor Nunn's film version of Shakespeare's *Twelfth Night.*

Alongside his film career, he has continued to appear in a number of notable BBC television productions, such as *Suddenly Last Summer, Hard Times, Karaoke,* and *A Royal Scandal.* His stage work includes a West End appearance in Nick Hytner's production of *The Importance of Being Earnest.*

Grant has recently published *With Nails,* a collection of reminiscences on his first ten years in movies.

Shelley Duvall

Shelley Duvall plays the Countess Gemini, Gilbert Osmond's eccentric sister.

Award-winning, multitalented actress-producer Shelley Duvall was discovered by producer Lou Adler and director Robert Altman while studying science in Houston, Texas.

Although she is probably best known for portraying Olive Oyl opposite Robin Williams in Altman's *Popeye* and Jack Nicholson's terrorized wife in Stanley Kubrick's *The Shining*, as chairman/CEO of Think Entertainment, Ms. Duvall is also well respected in the inner circle of the Hollywood community for being a pioneer in creating imaginative, entertaining, high-quality original programming for cable.

Ms. Duvall appeared regularly in the films of Robert Altman. Her first movie role was in *Brewster McCloud*. That was followed by five additional Altman films: *McCabe and Mrs. Miller, Thieves Like Us, Nashville, Buffalo Bill and the Indians,* and *Three Women,* for which she won the Best Actress Award at the Cannes Film Festival and the L.A. Critics' Award. She appeared in cameos in Woody Allen's *Annie Hall* and Terry Gilliam's *Time Bandits.* She also had a supporting role with Steve Martin in *Roxanne,* directed by Fred Schepisi. In late 1991, Ms. Duvall starred with Christopher Lloyd and Hulk Hogan in *Suburban Commando,* and has more recently appeared in Steven Soderbergh's *The Underneath.*

Ms. Duvall also produced and starred in *Mother Goose Rock 'n' Rhyme,* a ninety-minute musical movie for the Disney Channel. The program featured such talent as Paul Simon, Art Garfunkel, Bobby Brown, Cyndi Lauper, Debbie Harry, Little Richard, and Woody Harrelson. The film was honored with five ACE nominations and the Outstanding Children's Family Programming award.

Christian Bale

Christian Bale, who plays Pansy Osmond's suitor Edward Rosier, was most recently seen on our screens in Gillian

Armstrong's *Little Women* opposite Winona Ryder and Susan Sarandon.

Born in Wales, Christian received no formal training but made his West End theater debut at the age of ten in *The Nerd* with Rowan Atkinson.

He made his motion picture debut in Steven Spielberg's epic adaptation of J. G. Ballard's classic *Empire of the Sun*. The story of a young boy coming of age during the fall of Singapore in World War II garnered Christian rave reviews and the American Film Industry Committee gave him a special award "for an extraordinary performance by a juvenile actor."

Christian went on to co-star in Kenneth Branagh's version of Shakespeare's *Henry V* and in *Treasure Island* opposite Charlton Heston. Other screen performances include *Newsies*, *The Prince of Jutland*, directed by Gabriel Axel, and *Swing Kids* with Barbara Hershey and Kenneth Branagh. His television appearances include *Heart of the Country* and *A Murder of Quality* for the BBC.

Christian has a home in a beach town in southern California and he divides his time between there and Europe.

Viggo Mortensen

In Jane Campion's *The Portrait of a Lady*, Viggo Mortensen plays the role of Caspar Goodwood, Isabel Archer's unrelenting suitor.

One of America's most interesting young up-and-coming actors, Viggo Mortensen began his career in the theater, winning the Dramalogue Critics Award for his role of Captain in *Bent*. He began working in films in Peter Weir's *Witness* and won critical acclaim in Sean Penn's *Indian Runner*.

He has since worked with Brian De Palma (*Carlito's Way*), Tony Scott (*Crimson Tide*), and Danny Cannon (*Young Americans*), among others.

His most recent films include Kevin Spacey's *Albino Alligator* and Ridley Scott's *G.I. Jane*.

Valentina Cervi

Promising young Italian actress Valentina Cervi plays Pansy Osmond, Gilbert Osmond's obedient and apparently submissive daughter.

Valentina, twenty, was born in Rome and is the granddaughter of the popular Italian actor Gino Cervi, best known for playing the Communist mayor Peppone opposite the French comic Fernandel in the *Don Camillo* movies.

Valentina has appeared in a number of Italian movies since her debut in Carlo Cotti's *Portami la Luna* in 1986, notably Francesca Archibugi's *Mignon e Partita* and Sergio Rubini's *La Bionda*, with Nastassja Kinski. *The Portrait of a Lady* is her first English-language part. Valentina also speaks French and appears ready for an international career in European and American movies.

Jane Campion
Director and Scriptwriter

Born in Wellington, New Zealand, Jane Campion graduated with a Bachelor of Arts degree in anthropology from Victoria University of Wellington in 1975 and a Bachelor of Arts with painting major at Sydney College of Arts in 1979, where she began her filmmaking.

She attended the Australian Film, Television and Radio

School in the early 1980s. Here she wrote and directed her first short film, *Peel* (1982), which won the short film Palme d'Or at the Cannes Film Festival in 1986. Her other short films are *Passionless Moments* (1984), *A Girl's Own Story* (1983), *After Hours* (1984), and the telefeature *Two Friends* (1986), all of which won various Australian and international awards.

Campion went on to direct her first feature film, *Sweetie* (1989), which premiered in competition at Cannes and won the Georges Sadoul Prize in 1989 for Best Foreign Film, the L.A. Film Critics' New Generation Award in 1990, the American Independent Spirit Award for Best Foreign Feature, and the Australian Critics' Award for Best Film, Best Director, and Best Actress. She followed this with *An Angel at My Table* (1990), a dramatization based on the biographies of Janet Frame. This world-premiered at the Venice Film Festival in 1990, where it won seven awards, including the Silver Lion. It was also awarded prizes at Toronto and Berlin, again winning the American Independent Spirit Award, and was also voted the most popular film at the Sydney Film Festival in 1990.

The Piano (1992), written and directed by Campion, has received more than thirty international awards, including the Palme d'Or at the 1993 Cannes Film Festival and nine nominations at the 66th Academy Awards, picking up Best Screenplay, Best Actress, and Best Supporting Actress Oscars.